DOCUMENTS OF MODERN HISTORY

General Editors:

A. G. Dickens
The Director, Institute of Historical Research, University of London

Alun Davies
Professor of Modern History, University College, Swansea

THE DIPLOMACY OF
WORLD POWER:
THE UNITED STATES,
1889-1920

edited by

Arthur S. Link
Edwards Professor of American History, Princeton University

and

William M. Leary, Jr.
Assistant Professor of History, University of Victoria

St. Martin's Press
New York

CONTENTS

PREFACE

The record documenting the emergence of the United States as a decisive force in world affairs, from about 1889 to 1920, is so enormous that any selection of materials illustrating this momentous event must necessarily appear incomplete. However, we have tried to choose the landmark documents illustrating the major policies of the United States during this era.

The Introduction delineates the main contours and also provides the historical context of the documents in this volume. In addition, a brief introduction to each document illuminates its peculiar significance.

We trust that this book will prove helpful to students of modern diplomatic history as well as to that group of readers more particularly interested in exploring the foundations of American foreign policy in this century.

A. S. L.
W. M. L.

Princeton, New Jersey
May 21, 1968

INTRODUCTION

By the end of the nineteenth century, the United States was the greatest power in the world measured by any criteria – population, natural resources, or industrial might – except the availability of immediately disposable military and naval forces. But Americans, preferring to remain aloof, had chosen not to exercise their power abroad. 'Why,' Washington had asked, 'by interweaving our destiny with that of any part of Europe, entangle our peace and prosperity in the toils of European ambition, rivalship, interest, humour, or caprice?' Blessed by the broad expanses of the Atlantic and Pacific oceans, the great President's fellow-countrymen had yet, before the 1890s, to find a reason for the kind of embroilment that he had condemned.

American isolation, to be sure, had never been complete. Defence of the Monroe Doctrine had been a national objective, particularly since the resurrection of that policy by President Polk. Additionally, protection of its commerce had occasionally involved the United States in disputes with other nations. However, the Washington government, with no coherent foreign policy, apart from the Monroe Doctrine, had evidenced a monumental lack of concern about America's relations with the vast areas beyond the New World.

Profound changes, both domestic and foreign, were beginning to work a considerable leaven in American attitudes and policies by the end of the nineteenth century. The continental expansion of the United States was now substantially completed. The frontier, if not entirely closed, no longer absorbed the restless energies of the American people. Advances in technology were tending to nullify the advantages that the United States had so long enjoyed on account of its geographical insularity. Moreover, the American people were beginning to have a dim consciousness of their might and to believe that they were entitled to a voice in the councils of the world.

The 1890s, a time of depression and political unrest, marked the first movement of the United States on the world stage. The debut was, to say the least, awkward. Lacking any traditions in disposing international power, the country's course was erratic and frightening to established world powers. On occasion, the United States acted with bravado if not incivility in its dealings with other nations. For example, Secretary of State Richard Olney's note to Great Britain in 1895, asserting that the 'United States is practically sovereign on this continent, and its fiat is law upon the subjects to which it confines its interposition', could hardly have seemed to Whitehall as the proper language to use in addressing the foremost naval power (II, 1).

On the other hand, the tradition of non-involvement remained strong in the United States until well into the 1890s. In fact, President Cleveland's refusal to sanction the annexation of Hawaii in 1893 was undoubtedly more representative of American policy than were Olney's somewhat bombastic pronouncements (I, 1).

The United States crossed its Rubicon in 1898 with its decision to intervene in Cuba. Economic interest, strategic considerations, and domestic tensions were among the complex motives, but simple humanitarianism was probably the major factor in the decision to intervene. In the final analysis, it was American concern for the desperate plight of the Cuban people – a concern inflamed by lurid and often inaccurate stories in the press – that forced President McKinley to submit what was in fact a war message to Congress in April 1898 (I, 2).

The war with Spain was quick and relatively painless, but the consequences of the destruction of Spanish power around the world proved anything but painless. For the first time in its history since the War of 1812, the United States learned the important lesson that a nation cannot dispose power without incurring responsibilities. The debate among the peace commissioners in Paris mirrored the domestic controversy over one responsibility, the disposition of the Philippine Islands. In the end, the United States decided to assume control over territories and peoples far from American shores. Thus began a brief and disillusioning flirtation with imperialism (I, 4, 5, 6).

The crucial step had been taken. Isolationism was finished. On later occasions the United States would attempt to return to the halcyon period of non-involvement, but there was no way back. As President McKinley said in 1901, 'The period of exclusiveness is past' (I, 7).

Relations with Europe posed the least of the difficulties that the new America faced. An absence of conflicting national interests made for amicable if somewhat aloof relations with France and Germany. Only Great Britain stood as a potential threat to the vital interests of the United States.

The two English-speaking nations on the rim of the North Atlantic basin had many common interests and ties, but they also shared a heritage of hostility. Blood had been spilled during the Revolutionary War and the war of 1812, and the bitterness growing out of these conflicts had been kept alive during the nineteenth century by American politicians prone to 'twist the lion's tail' during election campaigns. For their part, the British tended to treat the upstart across the Atlantic with great and obvious disdain. Although Anglo-American relations were relatively calm after the settlement of issues growing out of the American Civil War, hostility, particularly anti-British hostility in the United States, was always just beneath the surface. It would break out on occasion, as during the Venezuelan boundary dispute (II, 1).

Yet leaders on both sides of the Atlantic saw mutual benefits in closer ties. The United States desired a free hand in the Western Hemisphere. Britain, isolated from the continental alliance system, wanted no enemy at its back. And there were visions of the great good that an Anglo-American partnership might accomplish in world affairs. Secretary of State John Hay, the leading proponent of this view (II, 2), was only one of a growing number of thoughtful Americans who shared it.

Several potential irritants to better Anglo-American relations remained by 1900, and the British were eager to remove them. With great understanding, and with greater patience, the festering controversies over fortification of the Panama Canal and the Alaskan boundary were resolved on American terms (II, 3, 4). A formal alliance was out of the question, given the traditional American abhorrence of such a commitment, but a firm, if ill-defined, Anglo-American understanding did take form between 1900 and 1914. Consequently, the word of the United States was indeed fiat in the western hemisphere by the latter date. Britain, in turn, won the increasing friendship of the American people, so much so that by 1914 probably a substantial majority of Americans were no longer basically anti-British.

Latin America, on account of its geographical proximity to the United States, became increasingly a sphere of influence of the United States as a result of the British decision no longer to challenge American supremacy in the southern reaches of the New World. Internal stability and non-interference by European powers were the two goals of United States policy in relations with neighbours to the south. As it happened, Latin America was one of the least stable areas in the world. Once the United States decided to construct an inter-oceanic canal, the Washington government became increasingly sensitive to Latin American instability, particularly in the Caribbean area.

The paternalistic and hegemonic character of American policy was clearly revealed in the Treaty with Cuba of 1903. Cuba, that document affirmed, was not to forfeit its independence to a foreign power. More important, the people of Cuba acknowledged the right of the United States to intervene in order to preserve domestic tranquillity in the island republic (**III, 1**). Relations between Latin American and European nations were also about to be put on a new basis. President Theodore Roosevelt, in his Annual Message of 1904, announced that the United States would hereafter act as an intermediary in conflicts between Latin American and European states, guaranteeing, among other things, payment of just debts (**III, 2**). That the United States was willing to assume the responsibilities enunciated in what was at once called the 'Roosevelt corollary' to the Monroe Doctrine was soon to be evidenced in the case of the Dominican Republic (**III, 3**).

Roosevelt, aware of the vulnerability of the Panama Canal, desired stability in Latin America primarily for reasons of high strategy. His successor, William Howard Taft, shared Roosevelt's concern but in the practical execution of policy emphasised financial and trade relations. Peaceful commercial intercourse, Taft believed, would benefit all nations in the Western Hemisphere. American intervention in the internal affairs of Latin American countries was not prompted by a desire to win special privileges but rather to protect the internal tranquillity necessary for trade and the development of the Latin American countries themselves (**III, 4**). Latin Americans failed to appreciate the subtleties of President Taft's motivations. In Latin American eyes, his policies at best constituted 'dollar diplomacy', at worst, 'Yankee imperialism'.

Woodrow Wilson, agreeing in large measure with the critics of United States policy toward Latin America, advocated a new approach. The United States would promote the growth of democratic institutions in countries to the south. The people of these countries, grateful for American assistance, would be tied forever in friendship to their northern neighbour (**III, 5**). The realities of Caribbean politics, however, soon made it extremely difficult for the President to realise his programme of helpfulness. Embroiled in Haiti (as in the Dominican Republic), Wilson thought that he had no recourse but to resort to military occupation (**III, 6**).

Mexico proved to be a thornier problem. Revolution, not ballots, brought new régimes to power there as in other Latin American countries. Wilson was determined to use all means short of war to support the principle of constitutional change through peaceful methods (**III, 7**). But American pressure only served to rally the Mexican people behind a beleaguered régime. In 1916 Mexico and the United States stood on the brink of hostilities. Faced with the possibility of war with Germany, Wilson proved just as determined to avert war with Mexico as he had been to support the principle of constitutional legitimacy (**III, 8**). Although the President's policy was based on altruistic motives and in the long run undoubtedly served the best interests of the Mexican people, the result of his policy was a heritage of bitterness between the two countries, particularly on the part of the Mexicans.

The Orient had had a peculiar lure for many Americans – merchants, missionaries, and adventurers – throughout the nineteenth century. Formal trade relations were established with China in the 1840s and it was an American squadron that had opened Japan to western commerce in the 1850s. American policy through this era was essentially that of the Open Door, that is, of maintaining a fair field with no favours. Only when this policy was endangered by the rise of Japan, the spread of European imperialism to China and the break-up of the Manchu Empire did the United States have occasion to articulate its objectives. Thus the Open Door notes of 1899 and 1900 represented no departure from American policy but rather were an attempt to maintain a *status quo* that had benefited American interests (**IV, 1, 2**).

The effort was doomed to failure in view of Japanese and European intentions and the needs of America's own merchants. In fact, the ink was scarcely dry on the Open Door note of 1900 before Secretary of State John Hay was seeking a coaling station on the coast of China. President Taft more realistically attempted to substitute a cooperative Open Door for a voluntary one. The objective – equal trade opportunities for all nations – remained unchanged, but it would be secured by a co-operative arrangement among the powers to share in major commercial and financial ventures in China (**IV, 7**). This policy also had proved completely unworkable even before Wilson delivered the *coup de grâce* to it in 1913 (**IV, 8**).

Japan was the key to relations with China and to stability in the entire Far East. Although American rhetoric was frequently expansionistic and jingoistic in tone (**IV, 4**), Washington evidenced an extraordinary degree of caution in dealing with the island Empire. The United States attempted to come to terms with Japanese power in a series of agreements, but to no avail (**IV, 5, 6, 9**). The failure and frustrations of American policy in the Far East were ably summarised in 1919 by the American Minister to China, Paul S. Reinsch (**IV, 10**). The United States was unable or unwilling either to define its goals in the

Orient or to agree on the means to achieve these ends. This problem would plague American policy for many years to come.

Difficulties in Latin America and the Far East paled into insignificance when compared to the crises and challenges to American policy-makers raised by the outbreak of war in Europe in 1914. The United States wanted only to protect its neutral maritime rights and to remain aloof from the European conflict (**V**, 1, 2, 6). As events turned out, this policy proved to be extraordinarily difficult. Britain, determined to take full advantage of superior seapower, instituted a strict blockade of the Central Powers. So long as this blockade conformed roughly to the canons of international law, the United States made no strong protest. But the British government's adoption of questionable practices, such as a broad definition of contraband and the extension of its blacklist to the United States, aroused Wilson's ire (**V**, 2, 3). Anglo-American controversy reached serious proportions during the summer of 1916. However, the British were careful not to push the United States to the brink of actual confrontation because they were so heavily dependent upon the United States for credits and war supplies.

The gravest danger to American neutral rights at sea came not from British maritime practices, which after all involved only property rights and could be adjudicated in the future, but from the challenge of the submarine. Wilson was not blind to the difficulties that submarine commanders faced in following traditional practices of 'visit and search'. The American President was willing to grant considerable latitude to the German government in the use of this new weapon. But Wilson drew the line sternly at the indiscriminate sinking of American ships (**V**, 4). He also thought that the sinking of unarmed passenger vessels, often with loss of American life, was intolerable. On several occasions, Wilson addressed sharp diplomatic protests to Berlin against what he said was illegal use of submarines (**V**, 5, 7). Only Wilson's determination to avoid belligerency if at all possible, and Germany's acquiescence in American demands, prevented war between the two countries before 1917.

Aside from the maintenance of American neutrality, Wilson's single great objective *vis-à-vis* the European belligerents from 1914 to 1917 was mediation in the war. However, neither the Allies nor the Central Powers could agree upon an acceptable basis for mediation. Both sides remained convinced that a military victory was possible and Wilson's effort failed (**VI**, 1, 2, 3).

In late January 1917, the Imperial German Government unleashed its augmented submarine force against all maritime commerce, belligerent and neutral. The Germans hoped to win the war quickly, by starving a Britain already teetering on the edge of economic disaster. The Imperial Government was willing to pay the price of American belligerency because it believed that American power could not be brought to bear in time to prevent German victory in Europe. Wilson had little choice but to go to war, but he did try to elevate the reasons for American entry from a legalistic defense of neutral rights into a crusade to construct a new world order dedicated to the prevention of war (**VI, 4**).

American military power was brought to bear in an unbelievably brief time and the tide of battle soon turned in favour of the Allies. Wilson's thoughts now more than ever turned to a peace of justice and reconciliation. The President developed specific proposals to implement a settlement of the war. Self-determination – the right of peoples to choose their own governments – was the heart of Wilson's programme (**VII, 1**). Autocratic governments, in his view, provoked wars; governments chosen by and responsible to their peoples would reflect the universal desire for peace. Thus Wilson had no enmity for the German people. However, he insisted that armistice and peace negotiations be conducted only with a régime responsible to the German people (**VII, 2**).

In spite of Wilson's great faith in humanity, his Calvinistic theology compelled him to realise that men were not perfect. Disputes between nations, even democratic nations, would inevitably arise. He therefore pressed for the formation of a concert of all nations to settle disputes and preserve the peace (**VII, 3, 4**). This concert, formalised as the League of Nations, became the keystone of Wilson's edifice; and at the heart of the League was Article X of the League's Covenant, or constitution (**VII, 5**).

Wilson won agreement for his League of Nations at the Paris Peace Conference of 1919, but only at the cost of compromises on several of his specific proposals. He did not consider these concessions too large a price to pay, for he was certain that the League would remove what he was the first to admit were certain injustices in the Treaty of Versailles ending the war with Germany.

Wilson did not fail at Paris, but he did fail to educate the American people in the realities of international life. Although opponents of the Treaty focused on such issues as Japan's violation of the principle of self-determination in the retention of Shantung Province, the controversy in the United States over ratification of the Versailles Treaty soon came to focus on the more crucial issue of America's participation in world affairs (**VII, 6**).

Wilson, predictably, took his case to the people (**VII 7**). But his nation-wide campaign was cut short by an incapacitating illness. He lost his battle for the League. The American people were unwilling to accept the far-reaching consequences and responsibilities that flowed from their possession of world power in 1919. This failure was a national, indeed an international, tragedy for which both the American people and President Wilson were responsible. The President, with sights too high, had demanded more than his people were willing to give. But Wilson's vision remains – a beacon that will shine so long as men search for peace.

I

IMPERIALISM AND THE
WAR WITH SPAIN

1 President Cleveland's Message to Congress regarding the Proposed Annexation of Hawaii, December 18, 1893

President Cleveland spoke for an older America in thwarting the movement to annex Hawaii in 1893. Not only would this act be 'a departure from unbroken American tradition', but the Provisional Government had seized power with American support and did not represent the wishes of the Hawaiian people. Cleveland, standing on the high ground of 'honor, integrity, and morality', successfully won his battle. But the expansionists were not to be denied for long. In the midst of the Spanish-American War, the United States annexed Hawaii.

To the Senate and House of Representatives

In my recent annual message to the Congress I briefly referred to our relations with Hawaii and expressed the intention of transmitting further information on the subject when additional advices permitted.

Though I am not able now to report a definite change in the actual situation, I am convinced that the difficulties lately created both here and in Hawaii and now standing in the way of a solution through Executive action of the problem presented, render it proper and expedient that the matter should be referred to the broader authority and discretion of Congress, with a full explanation of the endeavor thus far made to deal with the emergency and a statement of the considerations which have governed my action.

I suppose that right and justice should determine the path to be followed in treating this subject. If national honesty is to be disregarded and a desire for territorial extension, or dissatisfaction with a form of government not our own, ought to regulate our conduct, I have entirely misapprehended the mission and character of our Government and the behaviour which the conscience of our people demands of their public servants.

When the present Administration entered upon its duties the Senate had under consideration a treaty providing for the annexation of the Hawaiian Islands to the territory of the United States. Surely under our Constitution and laws the enlargement of our limits is a manifestation of the highest attribute of sovereignty, and if entered upon as an executive act all things relating to the transaction should be clear and free from suspicion. Additional importance attached to this particular treaty of annexation, because it contemplated a departure from unbroken American tradition in providing for the addition to our territory of islands of the sea more than 2,000 miles removed from our nearest coast.

These considerations might not of themselves call for interference with the completion of a treaty entered upon by a previous Administration. But it appeared from documents accompanying the treaty when submitted to the Senate, that the ownership of Hawaii was tendered to us by a Provisional Government set up to succeed the constitutional ruler of the islands, who had been dethroned, and it did not appear that such Provisional Government had the sanction of either popular revolution or suffrage. Two other remarkable features of the transaction naturally attracted attention. One was the extraordinary haste – not to say precipitancy – characterising all the transactions connected with the treaty. . . .

In the next place, upon the face of the papers submitted with the treaty, it clearly appeared that there was open and undetermined an issue of fact of the most vital importance. The message of the President accompanying the treaty declared that 'the overthrow of the monarchy was not in any way promoted by this Government,' and in a letter to the President from the Secretary of State, also submitted to the Senate with the treaty, the following passage occurs:

At the time the Provisional Government took possession of the Government buildings no troops or officers of the United States were present or took any part whatever in the proceedings. No public recognition was accorded to the Provisional Government by the United States minister until after the Queen's abdication and when they were in effective possession of the Government buildings, the archives, the treasury, the barracks, the police station, and all the potential machinery of the Government.

But a protest also accompanied said treaty, signed by the Queen and her ministers at the time she made way for the Provisional Government, which explicitly stated that she yielded to the supreme force of the United States, whose minister had caused United States troops to be landed at Honolulu and declared that he would support such Provisional Government.

The truth or falsity of this protest was surely of the first importance. If true, nothing but the concealment of its truth could induce our Government to negotiate with the semblance of a government thus created, nor could a treaty resulting from the acts stated in the protest have been knowingly deemed worthy of consideration by the Senate. Yet the truth or falsity of the protest had not been investigated.

I conceived it to be my duty therefore to withdraw the treaty from the Senate for examination, and meanwhile to cause an accurate, full, and impartial investigation to be made of the facts attending the subversion of the constitutional Government of Hawaii, and the installment in its place of the Provincial Government. . . .

I believe that a candid and thorough examination of the facts will force the conviction that the Provisional Government owes its existence to an armed invasion by the United States. Fair-minded people, with the evidence before them, will hardly claim that the Hawaiian Government was overthrown by the people of the islands, or that the Provisional Government has ever existed with their consent. I do not understand that any member of this Government claims that the people would uphold it by their suffrages if they were allowed to vote on the question.

While naturally sympathising with every effort to establish a republican form of government, it has been the settled policy of the United States to concede to people of foreign countries the same freedom and independence in the management of their domestic affairs that we have always claimed for ourselves; and it has been our practice to recognise revolutionary governments as soon as it became apparent that they were supported by the people. . . .

As I apprehend the situation, we were brought face to face with the following conditions:

The lawful Government of Hawaii was overthrown without the drawing of a sword or the firing of a shot by a process every step of which, it may safely be asserted, is directly traceable to and dependent for its success upon the agency of the United States acting through its diplomatic and naval representatives.

But for the notorious predilections of the United States minister for annexation, the committee of safety, which should be called the committee of annexation, would never have existed.

But for the landing of the United States forces upon false pretexts respecting the danger to life and property the committee would never have exposed themselves to the pains and penalties of treason by undertaking the subversion of the Queen's Government.

But for the presence of the United States forces in the immediate vicinity and in position to afford all needed protection and support the committee would not have proclaimed the Provisional Government from the steps of the Government building.

And finally, but for the lawless occupation of Honolulu under false pretexts by the United States forces, and but for Minister Stevens' recognition of the Provisional Government when the United States forces were its sole support and constituted its only military strength, the Queen and her Government would never have yielded to the Provisional Government, even for a time and for the sole purpose of submitting her case to the enlightened justice of the United States.

Believing, therefore, that the United States could not, under the circumstances disclosed, annex the islands without justly incurring the imputation of acquiring them by unjustifiable methods, I shall not again submit the treaty of annexation to the Senate for its consideration, and in the instructions to Minister Willis, a copy of which accompanies this message, I have directed him to so inform the Provisional Government.

But in the present instance our duty does not, in my opinion, end with refusing to consummate this questionable transaction. It has been the boast of our Government that it seeks to do justice in all things without regard to the strength or weakness of those with whom it deals. I mistake the American people if they favour the odious doctrine that there is no such thing as international morality, that there is one law for a strong nation and another for a weak one, and that even by direction a strong power may with impunity despoil a weak one of its territory.

By an act of war, committed with the participation of a diplomatic representative of the United States and without authority of Congress, the Government of a feeble but friendly and confiding people has been overthrown. A substantial wrong has thus been done which a due regard for our national character as well as the rights of the injured people requires we should endeavour to repair. The Provisional Government has not assumed a republican or other constitutional form, but has remained a mere executive council or oligarchy, set up without the assent of the people. It has not sought to find a permanent basis of popular support and has given no evidence of an intention to do so. Indeed, the representatives of that Government assert that the people of Hawaii are unfit for popular government and frankly avow that they can be best ruled by arbitrary or despotic power.

The law of nations is founded upon reason and justice, and the rules of conduct governing individual relations between citizens or subjects of a civilised State are equally applicable as between enlightened nations. The considerations that international law is without a court for its enforcement, and that obedience to its commands practically depends upon good faith, instead of upon the mandate of a superior tribunal, only give additional sanction to the law itself, and brand any deliberate infraction of it not merely as a wrong but as a disgrace. A man of true honor protects the unwritten word which binds his conscience more scrupulously, if possible, than he does the bond a breach of which subjects him to legal liabilities; and the United States, in aiming to maintain itself as one of the most enlightened of nations, would do its citizens gross injustice if it applied to its international relations any other than a high standard of honor and morality.

On that ground the United States can not properly be put in the position of countenancing a wrong after its commission any more than in that of consenting to it in advance. On that ground it can not allow itself to refuse to redress an injury inflicted through an abuse of power by officers clothed with its authority and wearing its uniform; and, on the same ground, if a feeble but friendly state is in danger of being robbed of its independence and its sovereignty by a misuse of the name and power of the United States, the United States can not fail to vindicate its honour and its sense of justice by an earnest effort to make all possible reparation.

These principles apply to the present case with irresistible force when the special conditions of the Queen's surrender of her sovereignty are recalled. She surrendered not to the Provisional Government, but to the United States. She surrendered not absolutely and permanently, but temporarily and conditionally until such time as the facts could be considered by the United States. Furthermore, the Provisional Government acquiesced in her surrender in that manner and on those terms, not only by tacit consent, but through the positive acts of some members of that Government who urged her peaceable submission, not merely to avoid bloodshed, but because she could place implicit reliance upon the justice of the United States, and that the whole subject would be finally considered at Washington.

I have not, however, overlooked an incident of this unfortunate affair which remains to be mentioned. The members of the Provisional Government and their supporters, though not entitled to extreme sympathy, have been led to their present predicament of revolt against the Government of the Queen by the indefensible encouragement and assistance of our diplomatic representative. This fact may entitle them to claim that in our effort to rectify the wrong committed some regard should be had for their safety. This sentiment is strongly seconded by my anxiety to do nothing which would invite either harsh retaliation on the part of the Queen or violence and bloodshed in any quarter.

In the belief that the Queen, as well as her enemies, would be willing to adopt such a course as would meet these conditions, and in view of the fact that both the Queen and the Provisional Government had at one time apparently acquiesced in a reference of the entire case to the United States Government, and considering the further fact that in any event the Provisional Government by its own declared limitation was only 'to exist until terms of union with the United States of America have been negotiated and agreed upon,' I hoped that after the assurance to the members of that Government that such union could not be consummated I might compass a peaceful adjustment of the difficulty.

Actuated by these desires and purposes, and not unmindful of the inherent perplexities of the situation nor of the limitations upon my power, I instructed Minister Willis to advise the Queen and her supporters of my desire to aid in the restoration of the status existing before the lawless landing of the United States forces at Honolulu on the 16th of January last, if such restoration could be effected upon terms providing for clemency as well as justice to all parties concerned. The conditions suggested, as the instructions show, contemplate a general amnesty to those concerned in setting up the Provisional Government and a recognition of all its bona fide acts and obligations. In short, they require that the past should be buried, and that the restored government should reassume its authority as if its continuity had not been interrupted. These conditions have not proved acceptable to the Queen, and though she has been informed that they will be insisted upon, and that, unless acceded to, the efforts of the President to aid in the restoration of her government will cease, I have not thus far learned that she is willing to yield them her acquiescence. The check which my plans have thus encountered has prevented their presentation to the members of the Provisional Government, while unfortunate public misrepresentations of the situation and exaggerated statements of the sentiments of our people have obviously injured the prospects of successful Executive mediation.

I therefore submit this communication with its accompanying exhibits, embracing Mr. Blount's report, the evidence and statements taken by him at Honolulu, the instructions given to both Mr. Blount and Minister Willis, and correspondence connected with the affair in hand.

In commending this subject to the extended powers and wide

discretion of the Congress, I desire to add the assurance that I shall be much gratified to co-operate in any legislative plan which may be devised for the solution of the problem before us which is consistent with American honor, integrity, and morality.

GROVER CLEVELAND

EXECUTIVE MANSION,
   Washington, December 18, 1893.
                    Congressional Record, 53rd Congress, 2nd
                    Session (December 18, 1893), pp. 309-12

2   President McKinley's Special Message to Congress regarding the Situation in Cuba, April 11, 1898

President McKinley also appealed to American tradition to justify intervention in Cuba. The 'interests of humanity', he believed, demanded such action. One can only glimpse in the President's message the emotional tides that surged through the United States in 1898. Public opinion had been roused to a fever pitch by lurid stories of Spanish atrocities in the popular press and inflammatory accounts of the sinking of U.S.S. *Maine.* The country wanted war; Congress wanted war. They were soon to have it.

To the Congress of the United States

Obedient to that precept of the Constitution which commands the President to give from time to time to the Congress information of the state of the Union and to recommend to their consideration such measures as he shall judge necessary and expedient it becomes my duty now to address your body with regard to the grave crisis that has arisen in the relations of the United States to Spain by reason of the warfare that for more than three years has raged in the neighbouring island of Cuba.

I do so because of the intimate connection of the Cuban question with the state of our own Union and the grave relation the course which it is now incumbent upon the nation to adopt must needs bear to the traditional policy of our Government if it is to accord with the precepts laid down by the founders of the Republic and religiously observed by succeeding Administrations to the present day.

The present revolution is but the successor of other similar insurrections which have occurred in Cuba against the dominion of Spain, extending over a period of nearly half a century, each of which, during its progress, has subjected the United States to great effort and expense in enforcing its neutrality laws, caused enormous losses to American trade and commerce, caused irritation, annoyance, and disturbance among our citizens, and, by the exercise of cruel, barbarous, and uncivilized practices of warfare, shocked the sensibilities and offended the humane sympathies of our people.

Since the present revolution began, in February, 1895, this country has seen the fertile domain at our threshold ravaged by fire and sword in the course of a struggle unequaled in the history of the island and rarely paralleled as to the numbers of the combatants and the bitterness of the contest by any revolution of modern times where a dependent people striving to be free have been opposed by the power of the sovereign state.

Our people have beheld a once prosperous community reduced to comparative want, its lucrative commerce virtually paralyzed, its exceptional productiveness diminished, its fields laid waste, its mills in ruins, and its people perishing by tens of thousands from hunger and destitution. We have found ourselves constrained, in the observance of that strict neutrality which our laws enjoin, and which the law of nations commands, to police our own waters and watch our own sea-ports in prevention of any unlawful act in aid of the Cubans.

Our trade has suffered; the capital invested by our citizens in Cuba has been largely lost, and the temper and forbearance of our people have been so sorely tried as to beget a perilous unrest among our own citizens which has inevitably found its expression from time to time in the National Legislature, so that issues wholly external to our own body politic engross attention and stand in the way of that close devotion to domestic advancement that becomes a self-contained commonwealth whose primal maxim has been the avoidance of all foreign entanglements. All this must needs awaken, and has, indeed, aroused the utmost concern on the part of this Government, as well during my predecessor's term as in my own.

In April, 1896, the evils from which our country suffered through the Cuban war became so onerous that my predecessor made an effort to bring about a peace through the mediation of this Government in any way that might tend to an honourable adjustment of the contest between Spain and her revolted colony, on the basis of some effective scheme of self-government for Cuba under the flag and sovereignty of Spain. It failed through the refusal of the Spanish Government then in power to consider any form of mediation or, indeed, any plan of settlement which did not begin with the actual submission of the insurgents to the mother country, and then only on such terms as

Spain herself might see fit to grant. The war continued unabated. The resistance of the insurgents was in no wise diminished.

The efforts of Spain were increased, both by the dispatch of fresh levies to Cuba and by the addition to the horrors of the strife of a new and inhuman phase happily unprecedented in the modern history of civilized Christian peoples. The policy of devastation and concentration, inaugurated by the Captain-General's bando of October 21, 1896, in the Province of Pinar del Rio was thence extended to embrace all of the island to which the power of the Spanish arms was able to reach by occupation or by military operations. The peasantry, including all dwelling in the open agricultural interior, were driven into the garrison towns or isolated places held by the troops.

The raising and movement of provisions of all kinds were interdicted. The fields were laid waste, dwellings unroofed and fired, mills destroyed, and, in short, everything that could desolate the land and render it unfit for human habitation or support was commanded by one or the other of the contending parties and executed by all the powers at their disposal.

By the time the present administration took office a year ago, reconcentration – so called – had been made effective over the better part of the four central and western provinces, Santa Clara, Matanzas, Habana, and Pinar del Rio.

The agricultural population to the estimated number of 300,000 or more was herded within the towns and their immediate vicinage, deprived of the means of support, rendered destitute of shelter, left poorly clad, and exposed to the most unsanitary conditions. As the scarcity of food increased with the devastation of the depopulated areas of production, destitution and want became misery and starvation. Month by month the death rate increased in an alarming ratio. By March, 1897, according to conservative estimates from official Spanish sources, the mortality among the reconcentrados from starvation and the diseases thereto incident exceeded 50 per centum of their total number.

No practical relief was accorded to the destitute. The overburdened towns, already suffering from the general dearth, could give no aid. So called 'zones of cultivation' established within the immediate areas of effective military control about the cities and fortified camps proved illusory as a remedy for the suffering. The unfortunates, being for the most part women and children, with aged and helpless men, enfeebled by disease and hunger, could not have tilled the soil without tools, seed, or shelter for their own support or for the supply of the cities.

Reconcentration, adopted avowedly as a war measure in order to cut off the resources of the insurgents, worked its predestined result. As I said in my message of last December, it was not civilized warfare; it was extermination. The only peace it could beget was that of the wilderness and the grave.

Meanwhile the military situation in the island had undergone a noticeable change. The extraordinary activity that characterized the second year of the war, when the insurgents invaded even the thitherto unharmed fields of Pinar del Rio and carried havoc and destruction up to the walls of the city of Havana itself, had relapsed into a dogged struggle in the central and eastern provinces. The Spanish arms regained a measure of control in Pinar del Rio and parts of Havana, but, under the existing conditions of the rural country, without immediate improvement of their productive situation. Even thus partially restricted, the revolutionists held their own, and their conquest and submission, put forward by Spain as the essential and sole basis of peace, seemed as far distant as at the outset.

In this state of affairs my Administration found itself confronted with the grave problem of its duty. My message of last December reviewed the situation and narrated the steps taken with a view to relieving its acuteness and opening the way to some form of honorable settlement. The assassination of the prime minister, Canovas, led to a change of government in Spain. The former administration, pledged to subjugation without concession, gave place to that of a more liberal party, committed long in advance to a policy of reform, involving the wider principle of home rule for Cuba and Puerto Rico.

The overtures of this Government, made through its new envoy, General Woodford, and looking to an immediate and effective amelioration of the condition of the island, although not accepted to the extent of admitted mediation in any shape, were met by assurances that home rule, in advanced phase, would be forthwith offered to Cuba, without waiting for the war to end, and that more humane methods should thenceforth prevail in the conduct of hostilities. Coincidentally with these declarations, the new Government of Spain continued and completed the policy already begun by its predecessor, of testifying friendly regard for this nation by releasing American citizens held under one charge or another connected with the insurrection, so that by the end of November not a single person entitled in any way to our national protection remained in a Spanish prison.

While these negotiations were in progress the increasing destitution of the unfortunate reconcentrados and the alarming mortality among them claimed earnest attention. The success which had attended the limited measure of relief extended to the suffering American citizens among them by the judicious expenditure through the consular agencies of the money appropriated expressly for their succor by the joint resolution approved May 24, 1897, prompted the humane extension of a similar scheme of aid to the great body of sufferers. A suggestion to this end was acquiesced in by the Spanish authorities. On the 24th of December last I caused to be issued an appeal to the American people, inviting contributions in money or in kind for the succor of the starving sufferers in Cuba, following this on the 8th of January by a similar public announcement of the formation of a central Cuban relief committee, with headquarters in New York City, composed of three members representing the American National Red Cross and the religious and business elements of the community.

The efforts of that committee have been untiring and have accomplished much. Arrangements for free transportation to Cuba have greatly aided the charitable work. The president of the American Red Cross and representatives of other contributory organizations have generously visited Cuba and cooperated with the consul-general and the local authorities to make effective distribution of the relief collected through the efforts of the central committee. Nearly $200,000 in money and supplies has already reached the sufferers and more is forthcoming. The supplies are admitted duty free, and transportation to the interior has been arranged so that the relief, at first necessarily confined to Havana and the larger cities, is now extended through most if not all of the towns where suffering exists.

Thousands of lives have already been saved. The necessity for a change in the condition of the reconcentrados is recognized by the Spanish Government. Within a few days past the orders of General Weyler have been revoked; the reconcentrados, it is said, are to be permitted to return to their homes and aided to resume the self-supporting pursuits of peace. Public works have been ordered to give them employment, and a sum of $600,000 has been appropriated for their relief.

The war in Cuba is of such a nature that short of subjugation or extermination a final military victory for either side seems impracticable. The alternative lies in the physical exhaustion of the one or the other party, or perhaps of both – a condition which in effect ended the ten years' war by the truce of Zanjon. The prospect of such a protraction and conclusion of the present strife is a contingency hardly to be contemplated with equanimity by the civilized world, and least of all by the United States, affected and injured as we are, deeply and intimately, by its very existence.

Realizing this, it appeared to be my duty, in a spirit of true friendliness, no less to Spain than to the Cubans who have so much to lose by the prolongation of the struggle, to seek to bring about an immediate termination of the war. To this end I submitted, on the 27th ultimo, as a result of much representation and correspondence, through the United States minister at Madrid, propositions to the Spanish Government looking to an armistice until October 1 for the negotiation of peace with the good offices of the President.

In addition, I asked the immediate revocation of the order of reconcentration, so as to permit the people to return to their farms and the needy to be relieved with provisions and supplies from the United States, cooperating with the Spanish authorities, so as to afford full relief.

The reply of the Spanish cabinet was received on the night of the 31st ultimo. It offered, as the means to bring about peace in Cuba, to confide the preparation thereof to the insular parliament, inasmuch as the concurrence of that body would be necessary to reach a final result, it being, however, understood that the powers reserved by the constitution to the central Government are not lessened or diminished. As the Cuban parliament does not meet until the 4th of May next, the Spanish Government would not object, for its part, to accept at once a suspension of hostilities if asked for by the insurgents from the general in chief, to whom it would pertain, in such case, to determine the duration and conditions of the armistice.

The propositions submitted by General Woodford and the reply of the Spanish Government were both in the form of brief memoranda, the texts of which are before me, and are substantially in the language above given. The function of the Cuban parliament in the matter of 'preparing' peace and the manner of its doing so are not expressed in the Spanish memorandum; but from General Woodford's explanatory reports of preliminary discussions preceding the final conference it is understood that the Spanish Government stands ready to give the insular congress full powers to settle the terms of peace with the insurgents – whether by direct negotiation or indirectly by means of legislation does not appear.

With this last overture in the direction of immediate peace, and its disappointing reception by Spain, the Executive is brought to the end of his effort.

In my annual message of December last I said:

Of the untried measures there remained only: Recognition of the insurgents as belligerents; recognition of the independence of Cuba; neutral intervention to end the war by imposing a rational compromise between the contestants, and intervention in favor of one or the other party. I speak not of forcible annexation, for that can not be thought of. That, by our code of morality, would be criminal aggression.

Thereupon I reviewed these alternatives, in the light of President Grant's measured words, uttered in 1875, when after seven years of sanguinary, destructive, and cruel hostilities in Cuba he reached the conclusion that the recognition of the independence of Cuba was impracticable and indefensible, and that the recognition of belligerence was not warranted by the facts according to the tests of public law. I commented especially upon the latter aspect of the question, pointing out the inconveniences and positive dangers of a recognition of belligerence which, while adding to the already onerous burdens of neutrality within our own jurisdiction, could not in any way extend our influence or effective offices in the territory of hostilities.

Nothing has since occurred to change my view in this regard, and I recognize as fully now as then that the issuance of a proclamation of neutrality, by which process the so-called recognition of belligerents is published, could, of itself and unattended by other action, accomplish nothing toward the one end for which we labor – the instant pacification of Cuba and the cessation of the misery that afflicts the island. ...

I said in my message of December last, 'It is to be seriously considered whether the Cuban insurrection possesses beyond dispute the attributes of statehood which alone can demand the recognition of belligerency in its favor.' The same requirement must certainly be no less seriously considered when the graver issue of recognizing independence is in question, for no less positive test can be applied to the greater act than to the lesser; while, on the other hand, the influences and consequences of the struggle upon the internal policy of the recognizing State, which form important factors when the recognition of belligerency is concerned, are secondary, if not rightly eliminable, factors when the real question is whether the community claiming recognition is or is not independent beyond peradventure.

Nor from the standpoint of expediency do I think it would be wise or prudent for this Government to recognize at the present time the independence of the so-called Cuban Republic. Such recognition is not necessary in order to enable the United States to intervene and pacify the island. To commit this country now to the recognition of any particular government in Cuba might subject us to embarrassing conditions of international obligation toward the organization so recognized. In case of intervention our conduct would be subject to the approval or disapproval of such government. We would be required to submit to its direction and to assume to it the mere relation of a friendly ally.

When it shall appear hereafter that there is within the island a government capable of performing the duties and discharging the functions of a separate nation, and having, as a matter of fact, the proper forms and attributes of nationality, such government can be promptly and readily recognized and the relations and interests of the United States with such nation adjusted.

There remain the alternative forms of intervention to end the war, either as an impartial neutral by imposing a rational compromise between the contestants, or as the active ally of the one party or the other.

As to the first it is not to be forgotten that during the last few months the relation of the United States has virtually been one of friendly intervention in many ways, each not of itself conclusive, but all tending to the exertion of a potential influence toward an ultimate pacific result, just as honorable to all interests concerned. The spirit of all our acts hitherto has been an earnest, unselfish desire for peace and prosperity in Cuba, untarnished by differences between us and Spain, and unstained by the blood of American citizens.

The forcible intervention of the United States as a neutral to stop the war, according to the large dictates of humanity and following many historical precedents where neighboring States have interfered to check the hopeless sacrifices of life by internecine conflicts beyond their borders, is justifiable on rational grounds. It involves, however, hostile constraint upon both the parties to the contest as well to enforce a truce as to guide the eventual settlement.

The grounds for such intervention may be briefly summarized as follows:

First. In the cause of humanity and to put an end to the barbarities, bloodshed, starvation, and horrible miseries now existing there, and which the parties to the conflict are either unable or unwilling to stop or mitigate. It is no answer to say this is all in another country, belonging to another nation, and is therefore none of our business. It is specially our duty, for it is right at our door.

Second. We owe it to our citizens in Cuba to afford them that protection and indemnity for life and property which no government there can or will afford, and to that end to terminate the conditions that deprive them of legal protection.

Third. The right to intervene may be justified by the very serious injury to the commerce, trade, and business of our people, and by the wanton destruction of property and devastation of the island.

Fourth, and which is of the utmost importance. The present condition of affairs in Cuba is a constant menace to our peace, and entails upon this Government an enormous expense. With such a conflict waged for years in an island so near us and with which our people have such trade and business relations; when the lives and liberty of our citizens are in constant danger and their property destroyed and themselves ruined; where our trading vessels are liable to seizure and are seized at our very door by war ships of a foreign nation, the expeditions of filibustering that we are powerless to prevent altogether, and the irritating questions and entanglements thus arising – all these and others that I need not mention, with the resulting strained relations, are a constant menace to our peace, and compel us to keep on a semiwar footing with a nation with which we are at peace.

These elements of danger and disorder already pointed out have been strikingly illustrated by a tragic event which has deeply and justly moved the American people. I have already transmitted to Congress the report of the naval court of inquiry on the destruction of the battle ship *Maine* in the harbour of Havana during the night of the 15th of February. The destruction of that noble vessel has filled the national heart with inexpressible horror. Two hundred and fifty-eight brave sailors and marines and two officers of our Navy, reposing in the fancied security of a friendly harbor, have been hurled to death, grief and want brought to their homes, and sorrow to the nation.

The naval court of inquiry, which, it is needless to say, commands the unqualified confidence of the Government, was unanimous in its conclusion that the destruction of the *Maine* was caused by an exterior explosion, that of a submarine mine. It did not assume to place the responsibility. That remains to be fixed.

In any event the destruction of the *Maine*, by whatever exterior cause, is a patent and impressive proof of a state of things in Cuba that is intolerable. That condition is thus shown to be such that the Spanish Government can not assure safety and security to a vessel of the American Navy in the harbor of Havana on a mission of peace, and rightfully there.

Further referring in this connection to recent diplomatic correspondence, a dispatch from our minister to Spain, of the 26th ultimo, contained the statement that the Spanish minister for foreign affairs assured him positively that Spain will do all that the highest honor and justice require in the matter of the *Maine*. The reply above referred to of the 31st ultimo also contained an expression of the readiness of Spain to submit to an arbitration all the differences which can arise in this matter, which is subsequently explained by the note of the Spanish minister at Washington of the 10th instant, as follows:

As to the question of fact which springs from the diversity of views between the reports of the American and Spanish boards, Spain proposes that the facts be ascertained by an impartial investigation by experts, whose decision Spain accepts in advance.

To this I have made no reply. . . .

The long trial has proved that the object for which Spain has waged the war can not be attained. The fire of insurrection may flame or may smolder with varying seasons, but it has not been and it is plain that it can not be extinguished by present methods. The only hope of relief and repose from a condition which can no longer be endured is the enforced pacification of Cuba. In the name of humanity, in the name of civilization, in behalf of endangered American interests which give us the right and the duty to speak and to act, the war in Cuba must stop.

In view of these facts and of these considerations, I ask the Congress to authorize and empower the President to take measures to secure a full and final termination of hostilities between the Government of Spain and the people of Cuba, and to secure in the island the establishment of a stable government, capable of maintaining order and observing international obligations, insuring peace and tranquillity and the security of its citizens as well as our own, and to use the military and naval forces of the United States as may be necessary for these purposes.

And in the interest of humanity and to aid in preserving the lives of the starving people of the island I recommend that the distribution of food and supplies be continued, and that an appropriation be made out of the public Treasury to supplement the charity of our citizens.

The issue is now with the Congress. It is a solemn responsibility. I have exhausted every effort to relieve the intolerable condition of affairs which is at our doors. Prepared to execute every obligation imposed upon me by the Constitution and the law, I await your action.

Yesterday, and since the preparation of the foregoing message, official information was received by me that the latest decree of the Queen Regent of Spain directs General Blanco, in order to prepare and facilitate peace, to proclaim a suspension of hostilities, the duration and details of which have not yet been communicated to me.

This fact with every other pertinent consideration will, I am sure, have your just and careful attention in the solemn deliberations upon which you are about to enter. If this measure attains a successful result, then our aspirations as a Christian, peace-loving people will be realized. If it fails, it will be only another justification for our contemplated action.

WILLIAM McKINLEY

EXECUTIVE MANSION, *April 11, 1898.*

> *Papers Relating to the Foreign Relations of the United States, 1898* (Washington, 1901), pp. 750–60.

3   Congressional Resolution regarding Cuba, April 20, 1898

It took Congress only nine days to authorise the President to employ American arms to secure Cuban independence. Section four of the Resolution – the Teller Amendment – reveals the high purposes of the United States.

[*Public Resolution—No. 21.*]

JOINT RESOLUTION for the recognition of the independence of the people of Cuba, demanding that the Government of Spain relinquish its authority and government in the island of Cuba, and to withdraw its land and naval forces from Cuba and Cuban waters, and directing the President of the United States to use the land and naval forces of the United States to carry these resolutions into effect.

Whereas the abhorrent conditions which have existed for more than three years in the island of Cuba, so near our own borders, have shocked the moral sense of the people of the United States, have been a disgrace to civilization, culminating as they have in the destruction of a United States battle ship, with two hundred and sixty-six of its officers and crew, while on a friendly visit in the harbor of Havana, and can not longer be endured, as has been set forth by the President of the United States in his message to Congress of April eleventh, eighteen hundred and ninety-eight, upon which the action of Congress was invited: Therefore,

Resolved by the Senate and House of Representatives of the United States of America in Congress assembled, First. That the people of the island of Cuba are, and of right ought to be, free and independent.

Second. That it is the duty of the United States to demand, and the Government of the United States does hereby demand, that the Government of Spain at once relinquish its authority and government in the island of Cuba, and withdraw its land and naval forces from Cuba and Cuban waters.

Third. That the President of the United States be, and he hereby is, directed and empowered to use the entire land and naval forces of the United States, and to call into the actual service of the United States the militia of the several States, to such extent as may be necessary to carry these resolutions into effect.

Fourth. That the United States hereby disclaims any disposition or intention to exercise sovereignty, jurisdiction, or control over said island, except for the pacification thereof, and asserts its determination, when that is accomplished, to leave the government and control of the island to its people.

Approved, *April 20, 1898.*

Papers Relating to the Foreign Relations of the United States, 1898 (Washington, 1901), p. 763

4. President McKinley's Instructions to the Peace Commissioners, September 16, 1898

The 'splendid little war' lasted less than four months. The United States scored a crushing military victory, attributable more to Spanish ineptitude than to the prowess of American arms. McKinley now considered the terms of peace.

EXECUTIVE MANSION,
Washington, September 16, 1898.

By a protocol signed at Washington August 12, 1898, a copy of which is herewith inclosed, it was agreed that the United States and Spain would each appoint not more than five Commissioners to treat of peace, and that the Commissioners so appointed should meet at Paris not later than October 1, 1898, and proceed to the negotiation and conclusion of a treaty of peace, which treaty should be subject to ratification according to the respective constitutional forms of the two countries.

For the purpose of carrying into effect this stipulation, I have appointed you as Commissioners on the part of the United States to meet and confer with Commissioners on the part of Spain.

As an essential preliminary to the agreement to appoint Commissioners to treat of peace, this Government required of that of Spain the unqualified concession of the following precise demands:

(1) The relinquishment of all claim of sovereignty over and title to Cuba.

(2) The cession to the United States of Porto Rico and other islands under Spanish sovereignty in the West Indies.

(3) The cession of an island in the Ladrones, to be selected by the United States.

(4) The immediate evacuation by Spain of Cuba, Porto Rico, and other Spanish islands in the West Indies.

(5) The occupation by the United States of the city, bay, and harbor of Manila pending the conclusion of a treaty of peace which should determine the control, disposition, and government of the Philippines.

These demands were conceded by Spain, and their concession was, as you will perceive, solemnly recorded in the protocol of the 12th of August.

By article 1 of that instrument Spain agreed to 'relinquish all claim of sovereignty over and title to Cuba.'

By article 2 she agreed to 'cede to the United States the island of Porto Rico and other islands now under Spanish sovereignty in the West Indies, and also an island in the Ladrones, to be selected by the United States.'

By article 3 it was declared that the United States would 'occupy and hold the city, bay, and harbor of Manila pending the conclusion of a treaty of peace which shall determine the control, disposition, and government of the Philippines.'

By article 4 provision was made for the immediate evacuation of Cuba, Porto Rico, and other Spanish islands in the West Indies, as follows:

Spain will immediately evacuate Cuba, Porto Rico, and other islands now under Spanish sovereignty in the West Indies; and to this end each Government will, within ten days after the signing of this protocol, appoint Commissioners, and the Commissioners so appointed shall, within thirty days after the signing of this protocol, meet at Habana for the purpose of arranging and carrying out the details of the aforesaid evacuation of Cuba and the adjacent Spanish islands; and each Government will, within ten days after the signing of this protocol, also appoint other Commissioners, who shall, within thirty days after the signing of this protocol, meet at San Juan, in Porto Rico, for the purpose of arranging and carrying out the details of the aforesaid evacuation of Porto Rico and other islands now under Spanish sovereignty in the West Indies.

The commissioners referred to in the foregoing article have been appointed, and they are now in session at Habana and San Juan, respectively. A copy of their instructions is herewith inclosed.

By these instructions you will observe that the evacuation of Cuba,

Porto Rico, and other Spanish Islands in the West Indies is treated as a military operation, and will, when carried into effect, leave the evacuated places in the military occupation of the United States. The purposes of the United States during such occupation are set forth in General Order No. 101 of the War Department of July 18, 1898, which was issued by direction of the President on the capitulation of the Spanish forces at Santiago de Cuba and in the eastern part of the Province of Santiago and the occupation of the territory by the forces of the United States. A copy of this order is hereto annexed for your information.

As the evacuation of Cuba and the other Spanish islands in the West Indies by the Spanish military forces devolves upon the United States the duty of taking possession of and holding and preserving all the immovable property therein previously belonging to the Government of Spain, the evacuation commissioners of the United States are instructed to arrange for the taking into possession and to take into possession for the United States, all public buildings and grounds, forts, fortifications, arsenals, depots, docks, wharves, piers, and other fixed property previously belonging to Spain, and to arrange for the care and safe-keeping of such property under the authority and control of the United States. Small arms and accouterments, batteries of field artillery, supply and baggage wagons, ambulances, and other impedimenta of the Spanish army in Cuba and other Spanish islands in the West Indies are to be removed, if desired, by the representatives of Spain, provided such removal shall be effected within a reasonable time; but the armament of forts, fortifications, and fixed batteries being in the nature of immovable fixtures, are not to be allowed to be taken, but are, in connection with such forts, fortifications, and batteries, to be taken over into the possession of the United States. The instructions of the evacuation commissioners also contain appropriate clauses in regard to the custody and preservation by the United States of state papers, public records, and other papers and documents necessary or convenient for the government of the islands, as well as all judicial and legal documents and other public records necessary or convenient for securing to individuals the titles to property.

It will be proper to confirm these transactions by appropriate clauses in the treaty of peace.

Similar clauses will be inserted in respect to the island ceded to the United States in the Ladrones. This Government has selected the Island of Guam, and you are instructed to embody in the treaty of peace a proper stipulation of cession.

A rumor has reached us from various quarters to the effect that the Spanish Peace Commissioners will be instructed to claim compensation for the public property of the Spanish Government in Cuba, as well as in territories agreed to be ceded to the United States. This rumor is not credited, but it is proper to make a few observations upon it. No such claim on the part of the Spanish Government is to be entertained in respect to any territory which Spain either cedes to the United States or as to which she relinquishes her sovereignty and title. The cession of territory or the relinquishment of sovereignty over and title to it is universally understood to carry with it the public property of the Government by which the cession or relinquishment is made. Any claim, therefore, on the part of Spain, such as that above suggested, would be inconsistent with the express agreements embodied in the protocol.

In the correspondence leading up to the signature of that instrument you will observe that this Government waived, for the time being, the requirement of a pecuniary indemnity from Spain. This concession was made in the hope that Spain would thereby be enabled promptly to accept our terms. But if the Spanish Commissioners should, contrary to our just expectations, put forward and insist upon a claim for compensation for public property, you are instructed to put forward as a counterclaim a demand for an indemnity for the cost of the war.

By article 6 of the protocol it was agreed that hostilities between the two countries should be suspended, and that notice to that effect should be given as soon as possible by each Government to the commanders of its military and naval forces. Such notice was given by the Government of the United States immediately after the signature of the protocol, the forms of the necessary orders having previously been prepared. But before notice could reach the commanders of the military and naval forces of the United States in the Philippines they captured and took possession by conquest of the city of Manila and its suburbs, which are therefore held by the United States by conquest as well as by virtue of the protocol.

In view of what has taken place it is necessary now to determine what shall be our future relations to the Philippines. Before giving you specific instructions on this subject it is my desire to present certain general considerations.

It is my wish that throughout the negotiations intrusted to the Commission the purpose and spirit with which the United States accepted the unwelcome necessity of war should be kept constantly in view. We took up arms only in obedience to the dictates of humanity and in the fulfillment of high public and moral obligations. We had no design of aggrandizement and no ambition of conquest. Through the long course of repeated representations which preceded and aimed to avert the struggle, and in the final arbitrament of force, this country was impelled solely by the purpose of relieving grievous wrongs and removing long-existing conditions which disturbed its tranquillity, which shocked the moral sense of mankind, and which could no longer be endured.

It is my earnest wish that the United States in making peace should follow the same high rule of conduct which guided it in facing war. It should be as scrupulous and magnanimous in the concluding settlement as it was just and humane in its original action. The luster and the moral strength attaching to a cause which can be confidently rested upon the considerate judgment of the world should not under any illusion of the hour be dimmed by ulterior designs which might tempt us into excessive demands or into an adventurous departure on untried paths. It is believed that the true glory and the enduring interests of the country will most surely be served if an unselfish duty conscientiously accepted and a signal triumph honorably achieved shall be crowned by such an example of moderation, restraint, and reason in victory as best comports with the traditions and character of our enlightened Republic.

Our aim in the adjustment of peace should be directed to lasting results and to the achievement of the common good under the demands of civilization, rather than to ambitious designs. The terms of the protocol were framed upon this consideration. The abandonment of the Western Hemisphere by Spain was an imperative necessity. In presenting that requirement, we only fulfilled a duty universally acknowledged. It involves no ungenerous reference to our recent foe, but simply a recognition of the plain teachings of history, to say that it was not compatible with the assurance of permanent peace on and near our own territory that the Spanish flag should remain on this side of the sea. This lesson of events and of reason left no alternative as to Cuba, Porto Rico, and the other islands belonging to Spain in this hemisphere.

The Philippines stand upon a different basis. It is none the less true, however, that, without any original thought of complete or even partial acquisition, the presence and success of our arms at Manila imposes upon us obligations which we can not disregard. The march of events rules and overrules human action. Avowing unreservedly the purpose which has animated all our effort, and still solicitous to adhere to it, we can not be unmindful that, without any desire or design on our part, the war has brought us new duties and responsibilities which we must meet and discharge as becomes a great nation on whose growth and career from the beginning the Ruler of Nations has plainly written the high command and pledge of civilization.

Incidental to our tenure in the Philippines is the commercial opportunity to which American statesmanship can not be indifferent. It is just to use every legitimate means for the enlargement of American trade; but we seek no advantages in the Orient which are not common to all. Asking only the open door for ourselves, we are ready to accord the open door to others. The commercial opportunity which is naturally and inevitably associated with this new opening depends less on large territorial possession than upon an adequate commercial basis and upon broad and equal privileges.

It is believed that in the practical application of these guiding principles the present interests of our country and the proper measure of its duty, its welfare in the future, and the consideration of its exemption from unknown perils will be found in full accord with the just, moral and humane purpose which was invoked as our justification in accepting the war.

In view of what has been stated, the United States can not accept less than the cession in full right and sovereignty of the island of Luzon. It is desirable, however, that the United States shall acquire the right of entry for vessels and merchandise belonging to citizens of the United States into such ports of the Philippines as are not ceded to the United States upon terms of equal favor with Spanish ships and merchandise, both in relation to port and customs charges and rates of trade and commerce, together with other rights of protection and trade accorded to citizens of one country within the territory of another. You are therefore instructed to demand such concession, agreeing on your part that Spain shall have similar rights as to her subjects and vessels in the ports of any territory in the Philippines ceded to the United States.

We are informed that numerous persons are now held as prisoners by the Spanish Government for political acts performed in Cuba, Porto Rico, or other Spanish islands in the West Indies, as well as in the Philippines. You are instructed to demand the release of these prisoners, so far as their acts have connection with matters involved in the settlement between the United States and Spain.

It will be desirable to insert in any treaty of peace which you may conclude a stipulation for the revival of the provisions of our former treaties with Spain, so far as they may be applicable to present conditions.

I have directed Gen. Wesley Merritt, the late commander at Manila, to report to the Commission at Paris, where he will arrive October 2, with such information as he may possess; and it is understood he will carry with him, for the use of the Commission, the views of Admiral Dewey. To the views of these distinguished officers I invite the most careful consideration of the Commission.

It is desired that your negotiations shall be conducted with all possible expedition, in order that the treaty of peace, if you should succeed in making one, may be submitted to the Senate early in the ensuing session. Should you at any time in the course of your negotiations desire further instructions, you will ask for them without delay.

WILLIAM MCKINLEY
Papers Relating to the Foreign Relations of the United States, 1898 (Washington, 1901), pp. 904-8

5   Division of Opinion among the Peace Commissioners with respect to the Disposition of the Philippine Islands, October 25, 1898

The disposition of the Philippines proved the thorniest issue at Paris. The Peace Commissioners could not agree on this question. The division of opinion in the American delegation mirrored similar divisions among the American people, who were already dividing into groups called imperialists and anti-imperialists. The following message to the President was from former Secretary of State William Rufus Day, head of the American peace commission.

Peace Commissioners to Mr. Hay
[Telegram.]

No. 16.]   *Paris, October 25, 1898.*
                              (Received on 25th and 26th.)
Differences of opinion among Commissioners concerning Philippines are set forth in statements transmitted herewith. On these we request early consideration and explicit instructions. Liable now to be confronted with this question in joint commission almost immediately.

DAY

Information gained by Commission in Paris leads to conviction that it would be naval, political, and commercial mistake to divide the archipelago. Nearly all expert testimony taken tends to this effect. As instructions provide for retention at least of Luzon, we do not consider question of remaining in Philippine Islands at all as now properly before us. We therefore ask for extension of instructions.

Spain governed and defended these islands from Manila; and with destruction of her fleet and surrender of her army we became as complete masters of the whole group as she had been, with nothing needed to complete the conquest save to proceed with the ample forces we had at hand to take unopposed possession. The Ladrones and Carolines were also governed from the same capital by the same governor-general.

National boundaries ought to follow natural divisions, but there is no natural place for dividing the Philippines.

There is hardly a single island in the group from which you can not shoot across to one or more of the others. Scarcely another archipelago in the world in which the islands are crowded so closely together and so interdependent. Military and naval witnesses agree that it would be practically as easy to hold and defend the whole as a part. Some say easier; all say safer. Agree, too, that ample and trustworthy military force could be raised among natives, needing only United States officers and a small nucleus of United States troops; also that islands could be relieved from oppressive Spanish taxation and yet furnish sufficient revenue for the whole cost of administration and defense.

Great danger must result from division. Other islands, seeing benefits from our government of Luzon, are sure to revolt, and to be aided and encouraged by natives of Luzon, thus repeating, in more aggravated form, our troubles with Spain about Cuba. Visayas already in revolt. Division would thus insure lawlessness and turbulence within gunshot of our shores, with no prospect of relief unless in Spanish sale of islands to unfriendly commercial rivals, which would probably happen if we hold the most important – Luzon – and release the others.

Generally expected now that this would be attempted the moment we released them. If such sale or transfer is to be made at all, would be less dangerous to our interests if done by us rather than by Spain. If we do not want the islands ourselves, better to control their disposition – i.e., to hold the option on them rather than to abandon it. Could then at least try to protect ourselves by ample treaty stipulations with the acquiring powers.

Commercially, division of archipelago would not only needlessly establish dangerous rivals at our door, but would impair value of part we kept. Present prosperity of Manila depends on its being natural center of import and export trade for the whole group. Large part of its business derived from Iloilo, Cebu, and other points in south. To yield these to unfriendly rivals would be to provide beforehand for diversion of business from our own possessions.

Moral obligations not to return Manila and Luzon to the oppressive power from which we have relieved them applies also to the rest of the archipelago, since Spanish power there is now broken and can not be restored without our consent. We believe public opinion in Europe, including that of Rome, expects us to retain whole of the Philippines, and would prefer that to any other solution save the impossible one of restoration of Spanish power over all the islands.

If a division should be insisted on, the only one that seems to us admissible would be by a line from the Straits of San Bernardino, south of Masbate and north of Panay, to the northeast corner of Borneo, leaving to the United States all to the westward, including Luzon, Mindoro, and Palawan. This would control the China Sea, and give excellent ports of call along the whole line from Borneo to Hongkong. But it would throw away the Visayas, including the best sugar, hemp, and tobacco islands. These contribute a large part of Manila's trade, and are inhabited generally by a people nearly as easy to manage as those of Luzon.

We are convinced that much injustice has been done inhabitants in published accounts of their character. Even the Mohammedans of Mindanao and the Sulu Archipelago, if left enjoyment of religious liberty and given freedom from oppressive taxation, would be found less intractable, in opinion of the experts, than under the rule of Spain; while the others would be comparatively easy to control, and glad to welcome strong and just rule of United States.

(Signed)   CUSHMAN K. DAVIS
WILLIAM P. FRYE
WHITELAW REID

(2) I am unable to agree that we should peremptorily demand the entire Philippine group. In the spirit of our instructions, and bearing in mind the often declared disinterestedness of purpose and freedom from designs of conquest with which the war was undertaken, we should be consistent in our demands in making peace. Territory permanently held must be taken as war indemnity, and with due regard to our responsibility because of the conduct of our military and naval authorities in dealing with the insurgents. Whether this conduct was wise or unwise is not now important. We can not leave the insurgents to mere treaty stipulations or to their unaided resources, either to form a government or to battle against a foe which, unequal to us, might readily overcome them. On all hands it is agreed that the inhabitants of the islands are unfit for self-government. This is particularly true of Mindanao and the Sulu group.

Only experience can determine the success of colonial expansion upon which the United States is entering. It may prove expensive in proportion to the scale upon which it is tried with ignorant and semi-barbarous people at the other side of the world. It should, therefore, be kept within bounds. Accepting Luzon, strategic advantage, as shown by high naval authority, may require cession of that part of the group lying north and west of a line drawn through San Bernardino Strait, south of Luzon to San Bernardino Islet, and thence by the Naranjos Islands and certain courses and distances to Tambisan Island, on the northeast coast of Borneo, conveying to the United States Luzon, Mindoro, Palawan, and various other islands, thus controlling the entrance to China Sea, with additional harbors and ports of call.

The objection that other islands will be acquired by European powers without regard to our interests can be obviated by treaty stipulation for nonalienation without the consent of the United States. There should also be stipulations for absolute freedom of trade and intercourse among all the islands of the group. This gives us practical control of the situation, with a base for the navy and commerce in the East, and responsibility for the people to whom we owe obligation and those most likely to become fit for self-government. It affords an opportunity for lessening the burden of colonial government, with room for further expansion if desired. It does not leave us open to the imputation of following agreement to negotiate with demand for whole subject-matter of discussion ourselves.

(Signed)   WILLIAM R. DAY

(3) The undersigned can not agree that it is wise to take Philippines in whole or in part. To do so would be to reverse accepted continental policy of country declared and acted upon throughout our history. Propinquity governs case of Cuba and Puerto Rico. Policy proposed introduces us into European politics and the entangling alliances against which Washington and all American statesmen have protested. It will make necessary a navy equal to largest of powers, a greatly increased military establishment, immense sums for fortifications and harbors, multiply occasions for dangerous complications with foreign nations, and increase burdens of taxation. Will receive in compensation no outlet for American labor in labor market already overcrowded and cheap, no area for homes for American citizens – climate and social conditions demoralizing to character of American youth. New and disturbing questions introduced into our politics, church question menacing. On whole, instead of indemnity – injury. Undersigned can

not agree that any obligation incurred to insurgents is paramount to our manifest interests. Attacked Manila as part of legitimate war against Spain. If we had captured Cadiz and Carlists had helped us, would not owe duty to stay by them at conclusion of war. On contrary, interest and duty would require us to abandon both Manila and Cadiz. No place for colonial administration or government of subject people in American system.

So much from standpoint of interest. But even conceding all benefits claimed for annexation, we thereby abandon the infinitely greater benefit to accrue from acting the part of a great, powerful, and Christian nation; we exchange the moral grandeur and strength to be gained by keeping our word to nations of the world and by exhibiting a magnanimity and moderation in hour of victory that becomes the advanced civilization we claim, for doubtful material advantages and shameful stepping down from high moral position boastfully assumed. We should set example in these respects, not follow in the selfish and vulgar greed for territory which Europe has inherited from mediæval times. Our declaration of war upon Spain was accompanied by a solemn and deliberate definition of our purpose. Now that we have achieved all and more than our object, let us simply keep our word. Third article of protocol leaves everything concerning control of Philippines to negotiation between the parties. Absurd now to say that we will not negotiate, but will appropriate whole subject-matter of negotiation. At the very least, let us adhere to President's instructions, and if conditions require the keeping of Luzon forego the material advantages claimed in annexing other islands – above all, let us not make a mockery of the injunction contained in those instructions, where, after stating that 'we took up arms only in obedience to the dictates of humanity and in the fulfilment of high public and moral obligations,' and that 'we had no design of aggrandizement and no ambition of conquest,' the President, among other things, eloquently says: 'It is my earnest wish that the United States in making peace should follow the same high rule of conduct which guided it in facing war. It should be as scrupulous and magnanimous in the concluding settlement as it was just and humane in its original action.' This and more, of which I earnestly ask a reperusal, binds my conscience and governs my action.

(Signed)   GEORGE GRAY

Papers Relating to the Foreign Relations of the United States, 1898 (Washington, 1901), pp. 932-5

6   Decision on the Philippines, October 28, 1898

McKinley faced up to the problem of the Philippines in late October 1898. His decision, dictated by the demands of 'duty', propelled the United States along the high road to world power. The following instruction from Secretary of State John Hay to Day embodied the President's decision.

Mr. Hay to Mr. Day

[Telegram.]

DEPARTMENT OF STATE,
Washington, October 28, 1898.

While the Philippines can be justly claimed by conquest, which position must not be yielded, yet their disposition, control, and government the President prefers should be the subject of negotiation, as provided in the protocol. It is imperative upon us that as victors we should be governed only by motives which will exalt our nation. Territorial expansion should be our least concern; that we shall not shirk the moral obligations of our victory is of the greatest. It is undisputed that Spain's authority is permanently destroyed in every part of the Philippines. To leave any part in her feeble control now would increase our difficulties and be opposed to the interests of humanity. The sentiment in the United States is almost universal that the people of the Philippines, whatever else is done, must be liberated from Spanish domination. In this sentiment the President fully concurs. Nor can we permit Spain to transfer any of the islands to another power. Nor can we invite another power or powers to join the United States in sovereignty over them. We must either hold them or turn them back to Spain.

Consequently, grave as are the responsibilities and unforeseen as are the difficulties which are before us, the President can see but one plain path of duty – the acceptance of the archipelago. Greater difficulties and more serious complications, administrative and international, would follow any other course. The President has given to the views of the Commissioners the fullest consideration, and in reaching the conclusion above announced, in the light of information communicated to the Commission and to the President since your departure, he has been influenced by the single consideration of duty and humanity. The President is not unmindful of the distressed financial condition of Spain, and whatever consideration the United States may show must come from its sense of generosity and benevolence, rather than from any real or technical obligation. The terms upon which the full cession of the Philippines shall be made must be left largely with the Commission. But as its negotiations shall proceed it will develop the Spanish position, and if any new phase of the situation arise, the Commission can further communicate with the President. How these instructions shall be carried out and whether to be presented as a peremptory demand, the President leaves to the judgment and discretion of the Commissioners.

HAY

Papers Relating to the Foreign Relations of the United States, 1898 (Washington, 1901), pp. 937-8

7   President McKinley on the Rise of the United States to World Power, September 5, 1901

The United States had taken the fatal step. A new era had dawned. McKinley, under whose auspices the change had occurred, realised the reasons why isolationism was no longer possible. But he did not live to see the consequences of his actions. He fell to an assassin's bullet on the day following this speech.

I am glad to be again in the city of Buffalo and exchange greetings with her people, to whose generous hospitality I am not a stranger, and with whose good will I have been repeatedly and signally honored. To-day I have additional satisfaction in meeting and giving welcome to the foreign representatives assembled here, whose presence and participation in this exposition have contributed in so marked a degree to its interest and success. To the commissioners of the Dominion of Canada and the British colonies, the French colonies, the republics of Mexico and of Central and South America, and the commissioners of Cuba and Porto Rico, who share with us in this undertaking, we give the hand of fellowship and felicitate with them upon the triumphs of art, science, education, and manufacture, which the old has bequeathed to the new century.

Expositions are the timekeepers of progress. They record the world's advancement. They stimulate the energy, enterprise and intellect of the people, and quicken human genius. They go into the home. They broaden and brighten the daily life of the people. They open mighty storehouses of information to the student. Every exposition, great or small, has helped to some onward step. Comparison of ideas is always educational; and as such instructs the brain and hand of man.

Friendly rivalry follows, which is the spur to industrial improvement, the inspiration to useful invention and to high endeavour in all departments of human activity. It exacts the study of the wants, comforts, and even the whims of the people, and recognizes the efficacy of high quality and new prices to win their favor. The quest for trade is an incentive to men of business to devise, invent, improve, and economize in the cost of production. Business life, whether among ourselves, or with other people, is ever a sharp struggle for success. It will be none the less so in the future. Without competition we would be clinging to the clumsy and antiquated processes of farming and manufacture and the methods of business of long ago, and the twentieth would be no further advanced than the eighteenth century. But though commercial competitors we are, commercial enemies we must not be.

The Pan-American Exposition has done its work thoroughly, presenting in its exhibits evidence of the highest skill and illustrating the progress of the human family in the Western Hemisphere. This portion of the earth has no cause for humiliation for the part it has performed in the march of civilization. It has not accomplished everything; far from it. It has simply done its best, and, without vanity or boastfulness, and recognizing the manifold achievements of others, it invites the friendly rivalry of all the powers in the peaceful pursuits of trade and commerce, and will co-operate with all in advancing the highest and best interests of humanity. The wisdom and energy of all the nations are none too great for the world's work. The success of art, science, industry, and invention is an international asset and a common glory.

After all, how near one to the other is every part of the world! Modern inventions have brought into close relation widely separated peoples and made them better acquainted. Geographic and political divisions will continue to exist, but distances have been effaced. Swift ships and fast trains are becoming cosmopolitan. They invade fields which a few years ago was [sic] impenetrable. The world's products are exchanged as never before, and with increasing transportation facilities come increasing knowledge and larger trade. Prices are fixed with mathematical precision by supply and demand. The world's selling prices are regulated by market and crop reports. We travel greater distances in a shorter space of time and with more ease than was ever dreamed of by the fathers. Isolation is no longer possible or desirable. The same important news is read, though in different languages, the same day in all Christendom. The telegraph keeps us advised of what is occurring everywhere, and the press foreshadows with more or less accuracy, the plans and purposes of the nations. Market prices of products and of securities are hourly known in every commercial mart, and the investments of the people extend beyond their own national boundaries into the remotest parts of the earth.

Vast transactions are conducted and international exchanges are made by the tick of the cable. Every event of interest is immediately bulletined. The quick gathering and transmission of news, like rapid transit, are of recent origin, and are only made possible by the genius of the inventor and the courage of the investor. It took a special messenger of the government, with every facility known at the time for rapid travel, nineteen days to go from the city of Washington to New Orleans with a message to General Jackson that the war with England had ceased, and that a treaty of peace had been signed. How different now.

We reached General Miles in Porto Rico by cable, and he was able through the military telegraph to stop his army on the firing line with the message that the United States and Spain had signed a protocol suspending hostilities. We knew almost instantly of the first shots fired at Santiago, and the subsequent surrender of the Spanish forces was known at Washington within less than an hour of its consummation. The first ship of Cervera's fleet had hardly emerged from that historic harbor when the fact was flashed to our capital, and the swift destruction that followed was announced immediately through the wonderful medium of telegraphy.

So accustomed are we to safe and easy communication with distant lands, that its temporary interruption, even in ordinary times, results in loss and inconvenience. We shall never forget the days of anxious waiting and awful suspense when no information was permitted to be sent from Peking, and the diplomatic representatives of the nations in China, cut off from all communication, inside and outside the walled capital, were surrounded by an angry and misguided mob that threatened their lives; nor the joy that thrilled the world when a single message from the Government of the United States brought, through our Minister, the first news of the safety of the besieged diplomats.

At the beginning of the nineteenth century there was not a mile of steam railroad on the globe. Now there are enough miles to make its circuit many times. Then there was not a line of electric telegraph; now we have a vast mileage traversing all lands and all seas.

God and man have linked the nations together. No nation can longer be indifferent to any other. And as we are brought more and more in touch with each other, the less occasion is there for misunderstandings and the stronger the disposition, when we have differences, to adjust them in the court of arbitration, which is the noblest forum for the settlement of international disputes.

My fellow citizens, trade statistics indicate that this country is in a state of unexampled prosperity. The figures are almost appalling. They show that we are utilizing our fields and forests and mines and that we are furnishing profitable employment to the millions of workingmen throughout the United States, bringing comfort and happiness to their homes, and making it possible to lay by savings for old age and disability. That all the people are participating in this great prosperity is seen in every American community, and shown by the enormous and unprecedented deposits in our savings banks. Our duty is the care and security of these deposits, and their safe investment demands the highest integrity and the best business capacity of those in charge of these depositories of the people's earnings.

We have a vast and intricate business built up through years of toil and struggle, in which every part of the country has its stake, which will not permit of either neglect, or of undue selfishness. No narrow, sordid policy will subserve it. The greatest skill and wisdom on the part of the manufacturers and producers will be required to hold and increase it. Our industrial enterprises which have grown to such great proportions affect the homes and occupations of the people and the welfare of the country. Our capacity to produce has developed so enormously, and our products have so multiplied that the problem of more markets requires our urgent and immediate attention. Only a broad and enlightened policy will keep what we have. No other policy will get more. In these times of marvelous business energy and gain we ought to be looking to the future, strengthening the weak places in our industrial and commercial systems, that we may be ready for any storm or strain.

By sensible trade arrangements, which will not interrupt our home production, we shall extend the outlets for our increasing surplus. A system which provides a mutual exchange of commodities is manifestly essential to the continued and healthful growth of our export trade. We must not repose in fancied security that we can forever sell everything and buy little or nothing. If such a thing were possible, it would not be best for us or for those with whom we deal. We should take from our customers such of their products as we can use without harm to our industries and labor. Reciprocity is the natural outgrowth of our wonderful industrial development under the domestic policy now firmly established. What we produce beyond our domestic consumption must have a vent abroad. The excess must be relieved through a foreign outlet, and we should sell everywhere we can, and buy whatever the buying will enlarge our sales and production, and thereby make a greater demand for home labor.

The period of exclusiveness is past. The expansion of our trade and commerce is the pressing problem. Commercial wars are unprofitable. A policy of good will and friendly trade relations will prevent reprisals. Reciprocity treaties are in harmony with the spirit of the times; measures of retaliation are not.

If perchance some of our tariffs are no longer needed, for revenue or to encourage and protect our industries at home, why should they not be employed to extend and promote our markets abroad? Then, too, we have inadequate steamship service. New lines of steamers have already been put in commission between the Pacific ports of the United States and those on the western coast of Mexico and Central and South America. These should be followed up with direct steamship lines between the Eastern coast of the United States and South American ports. One of the needs of the times is direct commercial lines from our vast fields of production to the fields of consumption that we have but barely touched.

Next in advantage to having the thing to sell is to have the convenience to carry it to the buyer. We must encourage our merchant marine.

We must have more ships. They must be under the American flag, built and manned and owned by Americans. These will not only be profitable in a commercial sense; they will be messengers of peace and amity wherever they go. We must build the Isthmian Canal, which will unite the two oceans and give a straight line of water communication with the Western coasts of Central and South America and Mexico. The construction of a Pacific cable cannot longer be postponed.

In the furtherance of these objects of national interest and concern, you are performing an important part. This exposition would have touched the heart of that American statesman whose mind was ever alert and thought ever constant for a larger commerce and a truer fraternity of the republics of the new world. His broad American spirit is felt and manifested here. He needs no identification to an assemblage of Americans anywhere, for the name of Blaine is inseparably associated with the Pan-American movement which finds this practical and substantial expression, and which we all hope will be firmly advanced by the Pan-American Congress that assembles this autumn in the capital of Mexico. The good work will go on. It cannot be stopped. These buildings will disappear; this creation of art and beauty and industry will perish from sight, but their influence will remain to

> 'Make it live beyond its too short living,
> With praises and thanksgiving.'

Who can tell the new thoughts that have been awakened, the ambitions fired and the high achievements that will be wrought through this exposition? Gentlemen, let us ever remember that our interest is in concord, not conflict, and that our real eminence rests in the victories of peace, not those of war. We hope that all who are represented here may be moved to higher and nobler effort for their own and the world's good, and that out of this city may come, not only greater commerce and trade for us all, but, more essential than these, relations of mutual respect, confidence, and friendship which will deepen and endure.

Our earnest prayer is that God will graciously vouchsafe prosperity, happiness, and peace to all our neighbors, and like blessings to all the peoples and powers of the earth.

The Last Speech of William McKinley, Delivered at the Pan-American Exposition, Buffalo, New York, on the Fifth of September 1901. Privately printed by the Kirgate Press, Canton, Pennsylvania, 1901

II

THE GROWTH OF ANGLO-AMERICAN FRIENDSHIP

I   Secretary Olney's Note regarding the Venezuelan Boundary Dispute, July 20, 1895

The Venezuelan boundary dispute provided the occasion for Secretary of State Richard Olney's long disquisition on the historical roots of American interest in South America. Behind Olney's rather broad interpretation of the Monroe Doctrine lay the reality of America's growing power. The British government, after some hesitation, recognised the fact of this power if not the logic of Olney's argument, and agreed to arbitration. The tribunal's decision was for the most part favourable to Britain.

Mr. Olney to Mr. Bayard

No. 804.]   DEPARTMENT OF STATE,
                                                 Washington, July 20, 1895.

His Excellency THOMAS F. BAYARD,
                        Etc., etc., etc., London.

SIR:

I am directed by the President to communicate to you his views upon a subject to which he has given much anxious thought and respecting which he has not reached a conclusion without a lively sense of its great importance as well as of the serious responsibility involved in any action now to be taken.

It is not proposed, and for present purposes is not necessary, to enter into any detailed account of the controversy between Great Britain and Venezuela respecting the western frontier of the colony of British Guiana. The dispute is of ancient date and began at least as early as the time when Great Britain acquired by the treaty with the Netherlands of 1814 'the establishments of Demerara, Essequibo, and Berbice.' From that time to the present the dividing line between these 'establishments' (now called British Guiana) and Venezuela has never ceased to be a subject of contention. The claims of both parties, it must be conceded, are of a somewhat indefinite nature. On the one hand Venezuela, in every constitution of government since she became an independent State, has declared her territorial limits to be those of the Captaincy General of Venezuela in 1810. Yet, out of 'moderation and prudence,' it is said, she has contented herself with claiming the Essequibo line – the line of the Essequibo River, that is – to be the true boundary between Venezuela and British Guiana. On the other hand, at least an equal degree of indefiniteness distinguishes the claim of Great Britain.

It does not seem to be asserted, for instance, that in 1814 the 'establishments' then acquired by Great Britain had any clearly defined western limits which can now be identified and which are either the limits insisted upon to-day, or, being the original limits, have been the basis of legitimate territorial extensions. On the contrary, having the actual possession of a district called the Pomaron district, she apparently remained indifferent as to the exact area of the colony until 1840, when she commissioned an engineer, Sir Robert Schomburgk, to examine and lay down its boundaries. The result was the Schomburgk line which was fixed by metes and bounds, was delineated on maps, and was at first indicated on the face of the country itself by posts, monograms, and other like symbols. If it was expected that Venezuela would acquiesce in this line, the expectation was doomed to speedy disappointment. Venezuela at once protested and with such vigor and to such purpose that the line was explained to be only tentative – part of a general boundary scheme concerning Brazil and the Netherlands as well as Venezuela – and the monuments of the line set up by Schomburgk were removed by the express order of Lord Aberdeen. Under these circumstances, it seems impossible to treat the Schomburgk line as being the boundary claimed by Great Britain as matter of right, or as anything but a line originating in considerations of convenience and expediency. Since 1840 various other boundary lines have from time to time been indicated by Great Britain, but all as conventional lines – lines to which Venezuela's assent has been desired but which in no instance, it is believed, have been demanded as matter of right. Thus neither of the parties is to-day standing for the boundary line predicated upon strict legal right – Great Britain having formulated no such claim at all, while Venezuela insists upon the Essequibo line only as a liberal concession to her antagonist. . . .

The important features of the existing situation, as shown by the foregoing recital, may be briefly stated.

(1) The title to territory of indefinite but confessedly very large extent is in dispute between Great Britain on the one hand and the

South American Republic of Venezuela on the other.

(2) The disparity in the strength of the claimants is such that Venezuela can hope to establish her claim only through peaceful methods – through an agreement with her adversary either upon the subject itself or upon an arbitration.

(3) The controversy, with varying claims on the part of Great Britain, has existed for more than half a century, during which period many earnest and persistent efforts of Venezuela to establish a boundary by agreement have proved unsuccessful.

(4) The futility of the endeavor to obtain a conventional line being recognized, Venezuela for a quarter of a century has asked and striven for arbitration.

(5) Great Britain, however, has always and continuously refused to arbitrate, except upon the condition of a renunciation of a large part of the Venezuelan claim and of a concession to herself of a large share of the territory in controversy.

(6) By the frequent interposition of its good offices at the instance of Venezuela, by constantly urging and promoting the restoration of diplomatic relations between the two countries, by pressing for arbitration of the disputed boundary, by offering to act as arbitrator, by expressing its grave concern whenever new alleged instances of British aggression upon Venezuelan territory have been brought to its notice, the Government of the United States has made it clear to Great Britain and to the world that the controversy is one in which both its honor and its interests are involved and the continuance of which it can not regard with indifference.

The accuracy of the foregoing analysis of the existing status cannot, it is believed, be challenged. It shows that status to be such that those charged with the interests of the United States are now forced to determine exactly what those interests are and what course of action they require. It compels them to decide to what extent, if any, the United States may and should intervene in a controversy between and primarily concerning only Great Britain and Venezuela and to decide how far it is bound to see that the integrity of Venezuelan territory is not impaired by the pretensions of its powerful antagonist. Are any such right and duty devolved upon the United States? If not, the United States has already done all, if not more than all, that a purely sentimental interest in the affairs of the two countries justifies, and to push its interposition further would be unbecoming and undignified and might well subject it to the charge of impertinent intermeddling with affairs with which it has no rightful concern. On the other hand, if any such right and duty exist, their due exercise and discharge will not permit of any action that shall not be efficient and that, if the power of the United States is adequate, shall not result in the accomplishment of the end in view. The question thus presented, as a matter of principle and regard being had to the settled national policy, does not seem difficult of solution. Yet the momentous practical consequences dependent upon its determination require that it should be carefully considered and that the grounds of the conclusion arrived at should be fully and frankly stated.

That there are circumstances under which a nation may justly interpose in a controversy to which two or more other nations are the direct and immediate parties is an admitted canon of international law. The doctrine is ordinarily expressed in terms of the most general character and is perhaps incapable of more specific statement. It is declared in substance that a nation may avail itself of this right whenever what is done or proposed by any of the parties primarily concerned is a serious and direct menace to its own integrity, tranquillity, or welfare. The propriety of the rule when applied in good faith will not be questioned in any quarter. On the other hand, it is an inevitable though unfortunate consequence of the wide scope of the rule that it has only too often been made a cloak for schemes of wanton spoliation and aggrandizement. We are concerned at this time, however, not so much with the general rule as with a form of it which is peculiarly and distinctively American. Washington, in the solemn admonitions of the Farewell Address, explicitly warned his countrymen against entanglements with the politics or the controversies of European powers.

Europe, [he said,] has a set of primary interests which to us have none or a very remote relation. Hence she must be engaged in frequent controversies the causes of which are essentially foreign to our concerns. Hence, therefore, it must be unwise in us to implicate ourselves by artificial ties in the ordinary vicissitudes of her politics or the ordinary combinations and collisions of her friendships or enmities. Our detached and distant situation invites and enables us to pursue a different course.

During the adminstration of President Monroe this Doctrine of the Farewell Address was first considered in all its aspects and with a view to all its practical consequences. The Farewell Address, while it took America out of the field of European politics, was silent as to the part Europe might be permitted to play in America. Doubtless it was thought the latest addition to the family of nations should not make haste to prescribe rules for the guidance of its older members, and the expediency and propriety of serving the powers of Europe with notice of a complete and distinctive American policy excluding them from interference with American political affairs might well seem dubious to a generation to whom the French alliance, with its manifold advantages to the cause of American independence, was fresh in mind.

Twenty years later, however, the situation had changed. The lately born nation had greatly increased in power and resources, had demonstrated its strength on land and sea and as well in the conflicts of arms as in the pursuits of peace, and had begun to realize the commanding position on this continent which the character of its people, their free institutions, and their remoteness from the chief scene of European contentions combined to give to it. The Monroe administration therefore did not hesitate to accept and apply the logic of the Farewell Address by declaring in effect that American non intervention in European affairs necessarily implied and meant European non-intervention in American affairs. Conceiving unquestionably that complete European non-interference in American concerns would be cheaply purchased by complete American non-interference in European concerns, President Monroe, in the celebrated Message of December 2, 1823, used the following language:

In the wars of the European powers in matters relating to themselves we have never taken any part, nor does it comport with our policy to do so. It is only when our rights are invaded or seriously menaced that we resent injuries or make preparations for our defense. With the movements in this hemisphere, we are, of necessity, more immediately connected, and by causes which must be obvious to all enlightened and impartial observers. The political system of the allied powers is essentially different in this respect from that of America. This difference proceeds from that which exists in their respective governments. And to the defense of our own, which has been achieved by the loss of so much blood and treasure and matured by the wisdom of their most enlightened citizens, and under which we have enjoyed unexampled felicity, this whole nation is devoted. We owe it, therefore, to candor and to the amicable relations existing between the United States and those powers to declare that we should consider any attempt on their part to extend their system to any portion of this hemisphere as dangerous to our peace and safety.

With the existing colonies or dependencies of any European power, we have not interfered and shall not interfere. But with the governments who have declared their independence and maintained it, and whose independence we have, on great consideration and on just principles, acknowledged, we could not view any inter-position for the purpose of oppressing them, or controlling in any other manner their destiny, by any European power, in any other light than as the manifestation of an unfriendly disposition towards the United States. . . . Our policy in regard to Europe, which was adopted at an early stage of the wars which have so long agitated that quarter of the globe, nevertheless remains the same, which is, not to interfere in the internal concerns of any of its powers; to consider the government *de facto* as the legitimate government for us; to cultivate friendly relations with it, and to preserve those relations by a frank, firm, and manly policy, meeting, in all instances, the just claims of every power, submitting to injuries from none. But in regard to these continents, circumstances are eminently and conspicuously different. It is impossible that the allied powers should extend their political system to any portion of either continent without endangering our peace and happiness; nor can anyone believe that our southern brethren, if left to themselves, would adopt it of their own accord. It is equally impossible, therefore, that we should behold such interposition, in any form, with indifference.

The Monroe administration, however, did not content itself with formulating a correct rule for the regulation of the relations between Europe and America. It aimed at also securing the practical benefits to result from the application of the rule. Hence the message just quoted declared that the American continents were fully occupied and were not the subjects for future colonization by European powers. To this spirit and this purpose, also, are to be attributed the passages of the same message which treat any infringement of the rule against interference in American affairs on the part of the powers of Europe as an act of unfriendliness to the United States. It was realized that it was futile to lay down such a rule unless its observance could be enforced. It was manifest that the United States was the only power in this hemisphere capable of enforcing it. It was therefore courageously declared nòt merely that Europe ought not to interfere in American affairs, but that any European power doing so would be regarded as antagonizing the interests and inviting the opposition of the United States.

That America is in no part open to colonization, though the proposition was not universally admitted at the time of its first enunciation, has long been universally conceded. We are now concerned, therefore, only with that other practical application of the Monroe doctrine the disregard of which by an European power is to be deemed an act of unfriendliness towards the United States. The precise scope and limitations of this rule cannot be too clearly apprehended. It does not establish any general protectorate by the United States over other American states. It does not relieve any American state from its obligations as fixed by international law nor prevent any European power directly interested from enforcing such obligations or from inflicting merited punishment for the breach of them. It does not contemplate any interference in the internal affairs of any American state or in the relations between it and other American states. It does not justify any attempt on our part to change the established form of government of any American state or to prevent the people of such state from altering that form according to their own will and pleasure. The rule in question has but a single purpose and object. It is that no European power or combination of European powers shall forcibly deprive an American state of the right and power of self-government and of shaping for itself its own political fortunes and destinies.

That the rule thus defined has been the accepted public law of this country ever since its promulgation cannot fairly be denied. Its pronouncement by the Monroe administration at that particular time was unquestionably due to the inspiration of Great Britain, who at once gave to it an open and unqualified adhesion which has never been withdrawn. But the rule was decided upon and formulated by the Monroe administration as a distinctively American doctrine of great import to the safety and welfare of the United States after the most careful consideration by a Cabinet which numbered among its members John Quincy Adams, Calhoun, Crawford, and Wirt, and which before acting took both Jefferson and Madison into its counsels. Its promulgation was received with acclaim by the entire people of the country irrespective of party. Three years after, Webster declared that the doctrine involved the honor of the country. 'I look upon it,' he said, 'as part of its treasures of reputation, and for one I intend to guard it,' and he added,

I look on the message of December, 1823, as forming a bright page in our history. I will help neither to erase it nor to tear it out; nor shall it be by any act of mine blurred or blotted. It did honor to the sagacity of the Government, and I will not diminish that honor.

Though the rule thus highly eulogized by Webster has never been formally affirmed by Congress, the House in 1864 declared against the Mexican monarchy sought to be set up by the French as not in accord with the policy of the United States, and in 1889 the Senate expressed its disapproval of the connection of any European power with a canal across the Isthmus of Darien or Central America. It is manifest that, if a rule has been openly and uniformly declared and acted upon by the executive branch of the Government for more than seventy years without express repudiation by Congress, it must be conclusively presumed to have its sanction. Yet it is certainly no more than the exact truth to say that every administration since President Monroe's has had occasion, and sometimes more occasions than one, to examine and consider the Monroe doctrine and has in each instance given it emphatic endorsement. Presidents have dwelt upon it in messages to Congress and Secretaries of State have time after time made it the theme of diplomatic representation. Nor, if the practical results of the rule be sought for, is the record either meager or obscure. Its first and immediate effect was indeed most momentous and far reaching. It was the controlling factor in the emancipation of South America and to it the independent states which now divide that region between them are largely indebted for their very existence. Since then the most striking single achievement to be credited to the rule is the evacuation of Mexico by the French upon the termination of the civil war. But we are also indebted to it for the provisions of the Clayton-Bulwer treaty, which both neutralized any interoceanic canal across Central America and expressly excluded Great Britain from occupying or exercising any dominion over any part of Central America. It has been used in the case of Cuba as if justifying the position that, while the sovereignty of Spain will be respected, the island will not be permitted to become the possession of any other European power. It has been influential in bringing about the definite relinquishment of any supposed protectorate by Great Britain over the Mosquito Coast.

President Polk, in the case of Yucatan and the proposed voluntary transfer of that country to Great Britain or Spain, relied upon the Monroe doctrine, though perhaps erroneously, when he declared in a special message to Congress on the subject that the United States could not consent to any such transfer. Yet, in somewhat the same spirit, Secretary Fish affirmed in 1870 that President Grant had but followed 'the teachings of all our history' in declaring in his annual message of that year that existing dependencies were no longer regarded as subject to transfer from one European power to another, and that when the present relation of colonies ceases they are to become independent powers. Another development of the rule, though apparently not necessarily required by either its letter or its spirit, is found in the objection to arbitration of South American controversies by an European power. American questions, it is said, are for American decision, and on that ground the United States went so far as to refuse to mediate in the war between Chili and Peru jointly with Great Britain and France. Finally, on the ground, among others, that the authority of the Monroe doctrine and the prestige of the United States as its exponent and sponsor would be seriously impaired, Secretary Bayard strenuously resisted the enforcement of the Pelletier claim against Hayti.

The United States, [he said,] has proclaimed herself the protector of this western world, in which she is by far the stronger power, from the intrusion of European sovereignties. She can point with proud satisfaction to the fact that over and over again has she declared effectively, that serious indeed would be the consequences if European hostile foot should, without just cause, tread those states in the New World which have emancipated themselves from European control. She has announced that she would cherish as it becomes her the territorial rights of the feeblest of those states, regarding them not merely as in the eye of the law equal to even the greatest of nationalities, but in view of her distinctive policy as entitled to be regarded by her as the objects of a peculiarly gracious care. I feel bound to say that if we should sanction by reprisals in Hayti the ruthless invasion of her territory and insult to her sovereignty which the facts now before us disclose, if we approve by solemn Executive action and Congressional assent that invasion, it will be difficult for us hereafter to assert that in the New World, of whose rights we are the peculiar guardians, these rights have never been invaded by ourselves.

The foregoing enumeration not only shows the many instances wherein the rule in question has been affirmed and applied, but also demonstrates that the Venezuelan boundary controversy is in any view far within the scope and spirit of the rule as uniformly accepted and acted upon. A doctrine of American public law thus long and firmly established and supported could not easily be ignored in a proper case for its application, even were the considerations upon which it is founded obscure or questionable. No such objection can be made, however, to the Monroe doctrine understood and defined in the manner already stated. It rests, on the contrary, upon facts and principles that are both intelligible and incontrovertible. That distance and three thousand miles of intervening ocean make any permanent political union between an European and an American state unnatural and inexpedient will hardly be denied. But physical and geographical considerations are the least of the objections to such a union. Europe, as Washington observed, has a set of primary interests which are peculiar to herself. America is not interested in them and ought not to be vexed or complicated with them. Each great European power, for instance, to-day maintains enormous armies and fleets in self-defense and for protection against any other European power or powers. What have the states of America to do with that condition of things, or why should they be impoverished by wars or preparations for wars with whose causes or results they can have no direct concern? If all Europe were to suddenly fly to arms over the fate of Turkey, would it not be preposterous that any American state should find itself inextricably involved in the miseries and burdens of the contest? If it were, it would prove to be a partnership in the cost and losses of the struggle but not in any ensuing benefits.

What is true of the material, is no less true of what may be termed the moral interests involved. Those pertaining to Europe are peculiar to her and are entirely diverse from those pertaining and peculiar to America. Europe as a whole is monarchical, and, with the single important exception of the Republic of France, is committed to the monarchical principle. America, on the other hand, is devoted to the exactly opposite principle – to the idea that every people has an inalienable right of self-government – and, in the United States of America, has furnished to the world the most conspicuous and conclusive example and proof of the excellence of free institutions, whether from the standpoint of national greatness or of individual happiness. It can not be necessary, however, to enlarge upon this phase of the subject – whether moral or material interests be considered, it can not but be universally conceded that those of Europe are irreconcilably diverse from those of America, and that any European control of the latter is necessarily both incongruous and injurious. If, however, for the reasons stated the forcible intrusion of European powers into American politics is to be deprecated – if, as it is to be deprecated, it should be resisted and prevented – such resistance and prevention must come from the United States. They would come from it, of course, were it made the point of attack. But, if they come at all, they must also come from it when any other American state is attacked, since only the United States has the strength adequate to the exigency.

Is it true, then, that the safety and welfare of the United States are so concerned with the maintenance of the independence of every American state as against any European power as to justify and require the interposition of the United States whenever that independence is endangered? The question can be candidly answered in but one way. The states of America, South as well as North, by geographical proximity, by natural sympathy, by similarity of governmental constitutions, are friends and allies, commercially and politically, of the United States. To allow the subjugation of any of them by an European power is, of course, to completely reverse that situation and signifies the loss of all the advantages incident to their natural relations to us. But that is not all. The people of the United States have a vital interest in the cause of popular self-government. They have secured the right for themselves and their posterity at the cost of infinite blood and treasure. They have realized and exemplified its beneficent operation by a career unexampled in point of national greatness or individual felicity. They believe it to be for the healing of all nations, and that civilization must either advance or retrograde accordingly as its supremacy is extended or curtailed. Imbued with these sentiments, the people of the United States might not impossibly be wrought up to an active propaganda in favor of a cause so highly valued both for themselves and for mankind. But the age of the Crusades has passed, and they are content with such assertion and defense of the right of popular self-government as their own security and welfare demand. It is in that view more than in any other that they believe it not to be tolerated that the political control of an American state shall be forcibly assumed by an European power.

The mischiefs apprehended from such a source are none the less real because not immediately imminent in any specific case, and are none the less to be guarded against because the combination of circumstances that will bring them upon us cannot be predicted. The civilized states of Christendom deal with each other on substantially the same principles that regulate the conduct of individuals. The greater its enlightenment, the more surely every state perceives that its permanent interests require it to be governed by the immutable principles of right and justice. Each, nevertheless, is only too liable to succumb to the temptations offered by seeming special opportunities for its own aggrandizement, and each would rashly imperil its own safety were it not to remember that for the regard and respect of other states it must be largely dependent upon its own strength and power. To-day the United States is practically sovereign on this continent, and its fiat is law upon the subjects to which it confines its interposition. Why? It is not because of the pure friendship or good will felt for it. It is not simply by reason of its high character as a civilized state, nor because wisdom and justice and equity are the invariable characteristics of the dealings of the United States. It is because, in addition to all other grounds, its infinite resources combined with its isolated position render it master of the situation and practically invulnerable as against any or all other powers.

All the advantages of this superiority are at once imperiled if the principle be admitted that European powers may convert American states into colonies or provinces of their own. The principle would be eagerly availed of, and every power doing so would immediately acquire a base of military operations against us. What one power was permitted to do could not be denied to another, and it is not inconceivable that the struggle now going on for the acquisition of Africa might be transferred to South America. If it were, the weaker countries would unquestionably be soon absorbed, while the ultimate result might be the partition of all South America between the various European powers. The disastrous consequences to the United States of such a condition of things are obvious. The loss of prestige, of authority, and of weight in the councils of the family of nations, would be among the least of them. Our only real rivals in peace as well as enemies in war would be found located at our very doors. Thus far in our history we have been spared the burdens and evils of immense standing armies and all the other accessories of huge warlike establishments, and the exemption has largely contributed to our national greatness and wealth as well as to the happiness of every citizen. But, with the powers of Europe permanently encamped on American soil, the ideal conditions we have thus far enjoyed can not be expected to continue. We too must be armed to the teeth, we too must convert the flower of our male population into soldiers and sailors, and by withdrawing them from the various pursuits of peaceful industry we too must practically annihilate a large share of the productive energy of the nation.

How a greater calamity than this could overtake us is difficult to see. Nor are our just apprehensions to be allayed by suggestions of the friendliness of European powers – of their good will towards us – of their disposition, should they be our neighbors, to dwell with us in peace and harmony. The people of the United States have learned in the school of experience to what extent the relations of states to each other depend not upon sentiment nor principle, but upon selfish interest. They will not soon forget that, in their hour of distress, all their anxieties and burdens were aggravated by the possibility of demonstrations against their national life on the part of powers with whom they had long maintained the most harmonious relations. They have yet in mind that France seized upon the apparent opportunity of our civil war to set up a monarchy in the adjoining state of Mexico. They realize that had France and Great Britain held important South American possessions to work from and to benefit, the temptation to destroy the predominance of the Great Republic in this hemisphere by furthering its dismemberment might have been irresistible. From that grave peril they have been saved in the past and may be saved again in the future through the operation of the sure but silent force of the doctrine proclaimed by President Monroe. To abandon it, on the other hand, disregarding both the logic of the situation and the facts of our past experience, would be to renounce a policy which has proved both an easy defense against foreign aggression and a prolific source of internal progress and prosperity.

There is, then, a doctrine of American public law, well founded in principle and abundantly sanctioned by precedent, which entitles and requires the United States to treat as an injury to itself the forcible assumption by an European power of political control over an American state. The application of the doctrine to the boundary dispute between Great Britain and Venezuela remains to be made and presents no real difficulty. Though the dispute relates to a boundary line, yet, as it is between states, it necessarily imports political control to be lost by one party and gained by the other. The political control at stake, too, is of no mean importance, but concerns a domain of great extent – the British claim, it will be remembered, apparently expanded in two years some 33,000 square miles – and, if it also directly involves the command of the mouth of the Orinoco, is of immense consequence in connection with the whole river navigation of the interior of South America. It has been intimated, indeed, that in respect of these South American possessions Great Britain is herself an American state like any other, so that a controversy between her and Venezuela is to be settled between themselves as if it were between Venezuela and Brazil or between Venezuela and Colombia, and does not call for or justify United States intervention. If this view be tenable at all, the logical sequence is plain.

Great Britain as a South American state is to be entirely differentiated from Great Britain generally, and if the boundary question cannot be settled otherwise than by force, British Guiana, with her own independent resources and not those of the British Empire, should be left to settle the matter with Venezuela – an arrangement which very possibly Venezuela might not object to. But the proposition that an European power with an American dependency is for the purposes of the Monroe doctrine to be classed not as an European but as an American state will not admit of serious discussion. If it were to be adopted, the Monroe doctrine would be too valueless to be worth asserting. Not only would every European power now having a South American colony be enabled to extend its possessions on this continent indefinitely, but any other European power might also do the same by first taking pains to procure a fraction of South American soil by voluntary cession.

The declaration of the Monroe message – that existing colonies or dependencies of an European power would not be interfered with by the United States – means colonies or dependencies then existing, with their limits as then existing. So it has been invariably construed, and so it must continue to be construed unless it is to be deprived of all vital force. Great Britain cannot be deemed a South American state within the purview of the Monroe doctrine, nor, if she is appropriating Venezuelan territory, is it material that she does so by advancing the frontier of an old colony instead of by the planting of a new colony. The difference is matter of form and not of substance and the doctrine if pertinent in the one case must be in the other also. It is not admitted, however, and therefore cannot be assumed, that Great Britain is in fact usurping dominion over Venezuelan territory. While Venezuela charges such usurpation, Great Britain denies it, and the United States, until the merits are authoritatively ascertained, can take sides with neither. But while this is so – while the United States may not, under existing circumstances at least, take upon itself to say which of the two parties is right and which wrong – it is certainly within its right to demand that the truth shall be ascertained. Being entitled to resent and resist any sequestration of Venezuelan soil by Great Britain, it is necessarily entitled to know whether such sequestration has occurred or is now going on. Otherwise, if the United States is without the right to know and have it determined whether there is or is not British aggression upon Venezuelan territory, its right to protest against or repel such aggression may be dismissed from consideration.

The right to act upon a fact the existence of which there is no right to have ascertained is simply illusory. It being clear, therefore, that the United States may legitimately insist upon the merits of the boundary question being determined, it is equally clear that there is but one feasible mode of determining them, viz., peaceful arbitration. The impracticability of any conventional adjustment has been often and thoroughly demonstrated. Even more impossible of consideration is an appeal to arms – a mode of settling national pretensions unhappily not yet wholly obsolete. If, however, it were not condemnable as a relic of barbarism and a crime in itself, so one-sided a contest could not be invited nor even accepted by Great Britain without distinct disparagement to her character as a civilized state. Great Britain, however, assumes no such attitude. On the contrary, she both admits that there is a controversy and that arbitration should be resorted to for its adjustment. But, while up to that point her attitude leaves nothing to be desired, its practical effect is completely nullified by her insistence that the submission shall cover but a part of the controversy – that, as a condition of arbitrating her right to a part of the disputed territory, the remainder shall be turned over to her. If it were possible to point to a boundary which both parties had ever agreed or assumed to be such either expressly or tacitly, the demand that territory conceded by such line to British Guiana should be held not to be in dispute might rest upon a reasonable basis. But there is no such line. The territory which Great Britain insists shall be ceded to her as a condition of arbitrating her claim to other territory has never been admitted to belong to her. It has always and consistently been claimed by Venezuela.

Upon what principle – except her feebleness as a nation – is she to be denied the right of having the claim heard and passed upon by an impartial tribunal? No reason nor shadow of reason appears in all the voluminous literature of the subject. 'It is to be so because I will it to be so' seems to be the only justification Great Britain offers. It is, indeed, intimated that the British claim to this particular territory rests upon an occupation, which, whether acquiesced in or not, has ripened into a perfect title by long continuance. But what prescription affecting territorial rights can be said to exist as between sovereign states? Or, if there is any, what is the legitimate consequence? It is not that all arbitration should be denied, but only that the submission should embrace an additional topic, namely, the validity of the asserted prescriptive title either in point of law or in point of fact. No different result follows from the contention that as matter of principle Great Britain cannot be asked to submit and ought not to submit to arbitration her political and sovereign rights over territory. This contention, if applied to the whole or to a vital part of the possessions of a sovereign state, need not be controverted. To hold otherwise might be equivalent to holding that a sovereign state was bound to arbitrate its very existence.

But Great Britain has herself shown in various instances that the principle has no pertinency when either the interests or the territorial area involved are not of controlling magnitude and her loss of them as the result of an arbitration cannot appreciably affect her honor or her power. Thus, she has arbitrated the extent of her colonial possessions twice with the United States, twice with Portugal, and once with Germany, and perhaps in other instances. The Northwest Water Boundary arbitration of 1872 between her and this country is an example in point and well illustrates both the effect to be given to long-continued use and enjoyment and the fact that a truly great power sacrifices neither prestige nor dignity by reconsidering the most emphatic rejection of a proposition when satisfied of the obvious and intrinsic justice of the case. By the award of the Emperor of Germany, the arbitrator in that case, the United States acquired San Juan and a number of smaller islands near the coast of Vancouver as a consequence of the decision that the term 'the channel which separates the continent from Vancouver's Island,' as used in the treaty of Washington of 1846, meant the Haro channel and not the Rosario channel. Yet a leading contention of Great Britain before the arbitrator was that equity required a judgment in her favor because a decision in favor of the United States would deprive British subjects of rights of navigation of which they had had the habitual enjoyment from the time when the Rosario Strait was first explored and surveyed in 1798. So, though by virtue of the award the United States acquired San Juan and the other islands of the group to which it belongs, the British Foreign Secretary had in 1859 instructed the British Minister at Washington as follows:

> Her Majesty's Government must, therefore, under any circumstances, maintain the right of the British Crown to the Island of San Juan. The interests at stake in connection with the retention of that Island are too important to admit of compromise and Your Lordship will consequently bear in mind that, whatever arrangement as to the boundary line is finally arrived at, no settlement of the question will be accepted by Her Majesty's Government which does not provide for the Island of San Juan being reserved to the British Crown.

Thus, as already intimated, the British demand that her right to a portion of the disputed territory shall be acknowledged before she will consent to an arbitration as to the rest seems to stand upon nothing but her own *ipse dixit*. She says to Venezuela, in substance: 'You can get none of the debatable land by force, because you are not strong enough; you can get none by treaty, because I will not agree; and you can take your chance of getting a portion by arbitration, only if you first agree to abandon to me such other portion as I may designate.' It is not perceived how such an attitude can be defended nor how it is reconcilable with that love of justice and fair play so eminently characteristic of the English race. It in effect deprives Venezuela of her free agency and puts her under virtual duress. Territory acquired by reason of it will be as much wrested from her by the strong hand as if occupied by British troops or covered by British fleets. It seems therefore quite impossible that this position of Great Britain should be assented to by the United States, or that, if such position be adhered to with the result of enlarging the bounds of British Guiana, it should not be regarded as amounting, in substance, to an invasion and conquest of Venezuelan territory.

In these circumstances, the duty of the President appears to him unmistakable and imperative. Great Britain's assertion of title to the disputed territory combined with her refusal to have that title investigated being a substantial appropriation of the territory to her own use, not to protest and give warning that the transaction will be regarded as injurious to the interests of the people of the United States as well as oppressive in itself would be to ignore an established policy with which the honor and welfare of this country are closely identified. While the measures necessary or proper for the vindication of that policy are to be determined by another branch of the Government, it is clearly for the Executive to leave nothing undone which may tend to render such determination unnecessary.

You are instructed, therefore, to present the foregoing views to Lord Salisbury by reading to him this communication (leaving with him a copy should he so desire), and to reinforce them by such pertinent considerations as will doubtless occur to you. They call for a definite decision upon the point whether Great Britain will consent or will decline to submit the Venezuelan boundary question in its entirety to impartial arbitration. It is the earnest hope of the President that the conclusion will be on the side of arbitration, and that Great Britain will add one more to the conspicuous precedents she has already furnished in favor of that wise and just mode of adjusting international disputes. If he is to be disappointed in that hope, however – a result not to be anticipated and in his judgment calculated to greatly embarrass the future relations between this country and Great Britain – it is his wish to be made acquainted with the fact at such early date as will enable him to lay the whole subject before Congress in his next annual message.

I am, sir, your obedient servant,

RICHARD OLNEY

Papers Relating to the Foreign Relations of the United States, 1895 (2 parts, Washington, 1896), Part I, pp. 545-62

2   John Hay on Anglo-American Friendship, April 21, 1898

Secretary Hay, a leading advocate of Anglo-American friendship, worked diligently for closer ties between the two English-speaking peoples. On many occasions, the following, for example, he described in the most glowing terms the mutual benefits to be derived from such a partnership.

I am honored in having the privilege of thanking you, on behalf of all my colleagues as well as myself, and the countries which we represent, for the cordiality with which this toast has been proposed and the kindness with which it has been received. In this place, the civic heart of London, the home of a traditional and princely hospitality, whence from time immemorial the only challenge that has gone forth has been one inviting the world to that wholesome competition in civilizing arts which benefits all parties to it, we cannot but accept this courtesy in the spirit in which it is tendered, and in return wish success and prosperity to England and to British trade and commerce, in the full assurance that all the nations of the world will profit more or less directly by every extension of British commerce and the enterprise and enlightenment that go with it hand-in-hand.

Perhaps I may be pardoned if I say a word about my own country. Knitted as we are to the people of Great Britain by a thousand ties, of origin, of language, and of kindred pursuits, it is inevitable that from time to time we should have occasions of discussion and even of difference. We hear sometimes that we are thought to be somewhat eager and pertinacious in the pursuit of our own interests. If that is so, I can say, I hope with no impertinence, and in a spirit rather of pride than of contrition, that it merely goes to show of what stock we are. But this truth is unquestionable – that for now nearly three generations of men there has been peace between us and friendly regard, a peace growing more solid and durable as years go by, and a friendship that I am sure the vast majority of both peoples hope and trust is to be eternal. The reasons of a good understanding between us lie deeper than any considerations of mere expediency. All of us who think cannot but see that there is a sanction like that of religion which binds us to a sort of partnership in the beneficent work of the world. Whether we will it or not, we are associated in that work by the very nature of things, and no man and no group of men can prevent it. We are bound by a tie which we did not forge and which we cannot break; we are joint ministers of the same sacred mission of liberty and progress, charged with duties which we cannot evade by the imposition of irresistible hands.

It may be trite and even tedious for me to refer again at this distance of time to the mighty pageant of last June, but I may ask leave to recall one incident of the naval review, which will long be remembered by those who saw it. On the evening of that memorable day, when all the ships lay enshrouded in darkness, the commander of the *Brooklyn* ran up the British and American colors, and then at a given signal turned upon those two kindred flags the brilliant rays of her searchlights. In that high illumination shrined in clear radiance far above the obscurity that hid the engines of destruction and preparations for war, those friendly banners fluttered, proclaiming to the navies of the world their message of good will. The beauty of the scene lasted but a moment; it passed away with much of the splendor and magnificence that adorned the historic day; but may we not hope that the lesson and the inspiration of that spectacle may last as long as those banners shall float over the seven seas, carrying always in their shadow freedom and civilization?

> 'A Partnership in Beneficence: Speech at Easter Banquet, Mansion House, London, April 21, 1898', *Addresses of John Hay* (New York, 1907), pp. 77-80

3   The Hay-Pauncefote Treaty, November 18, 1901

The Spanish-American War imparted a sense of urgency to the long-standing American desire to construct an inter-ocean canal. Under the terms of the Clayton-Bulwer Treaty of 1850, the United States and Great Britain had agreed to a neutralised and unfortified canal to be constructed by both nations. Washington now found these stipulations unsatisfactory. The first Hay-Pauncefote Treaty was negotiated in 1900. Britain generously consented to exclusive American control over the proposed canal, but the provision for non-fortification remained. When Congress found this unacceptable, Britain agreed to re-negotiate the treaty. Although the second Hay-Pauncefote Treaty of 1901 left out any mention of fortification, the British government conceded this right to the United States in a separate memorandum. Great Britain, clearly, was prepared to go to extraordinary lengths to secure American friendship.

TREATY TO FACILITATE THE CONSTRUCTION OF A SHIP CANAL
Concluded November 18, 1901; ratification advised by Senate December 16, 1901; ratified by President December 26, 1901; ratifications exchanged February 21, 1902; proclaimed February 22, 1902

ARTICLES

I   Convention of April 19, 1850   IV Change of sovereignty
II Construction of canal   V   Ratification
III Rules of neutralization

The United States of America and His Majesty Edward the Seventh, of the United Kingdom of Great Britain and Ireland, and of the British Dominions beyond the Seas, King, and Emperor of India, being desirous to facilitate the construction of a ship canal to connect the Atlantic and Pacific Oceans, by whatever route may be considered expedient, and to that end to remove any objection which may arise out of the Convention of the 19th April, 1850, commonly called the Clayton-Bulwer Treaty, to the construction of such canal under the auspices of the Government of the United States, without impairing the 'general principle' of neutralization established in Article VIII of that Convention, have for that purpose appointed as their Plenipotentiaries:

The President of the United States, John Hay, Secretary of State of the United States of America;

And His Majesty Edward the Seventh, of the United Kingdom of Great Britain and Ireland, and of the British Dominions beyond the Seas, King, and Emperor of India, the Right Honourable Lord Paunce-fote, G.C.B., G.C.M.G., His Majesty's Ambassador Extraordinary and Plenipotentiary to the United States;

Who, having communicated to each other their full powers which were found to be in due and proper form, have agreed upon the following Articles:–

Article I

The High Contracting Parties agree that the present Treaty shall supersede the afore-mentioned Convention of the 19th April, 1850.

Article II

It is agreed that the canal may be constructed under the auspices of the Government of the United States, either directly at its own cost, or by gift or loan of money to individuals or Corporations, or through subscription to or purchase of stock or shares, and that, subject to the provisions of the present Treaty, the said Government shall have and enjoy all the rights incident to such construction, as well as the exclusive right of providing for the regulation and management of the canal.

Article III

The United States adopts, as the basis of the neutralization of such ship canal, the following Rules, substantially as embodied in the Convention of Constantinople, signed the 28th October, 1888, for the free navigation of the Suez Canal, that is to say:

(1) The canal shall be free and open to the vessels of commerce and of war of all nations observing these Rules, on terms of entire equality, so that there shall be no discrimination against any such nation, or its citizens or subjects, in respect of the conditions or charges of traffic, or otherwise. Such conditions and charges of traffic shall be just and equitable.

(2) The canal shall never be blockaded, nor shall any right of war be

exercised nor any act of hostility be committed within it. The United'
States, however, shall be at liberty to maintain such military police along
the canal as may be necessary to protect it against lawlessness and disorder.

(3) Vessels of war of a belligerent shall not revictual nor take any
stores in the canal except so far as may be strictly necessary; and the
transit of such vessels through the canal shall be effected with the least
possible delay in accordance with the Regulations in force, and with
only such intermission as may result from the necessities of the service.

Prizes shall be in all respects subject to the same Rules as vessels of war
of the belligerents.

(4) No belligerent shall embark or disembark troops, munitions of
war, or warlike materials in the canal, except in case of accidental
hindrance of the transit, and in such case the transit shall be resumed
with all possible dispatch.

(5) The provisions of this Article shall apply to waters adjacent to the
canal, within 3 marine miles of either end. Vessels of war of a belligerent
shall not remain in such waters longer than twenty-four hours at any
one time, except in case of distress, and in such case, shall depart as soon
as possible; but a vessel of war of one belligerent shall not depart within
twenty-four hours from the departure of a vessel of war of the other
belligerent.

(6) The plant, establishments, buildings, and all work necessary to
the construction, maintenance, and operation of the canal shall be
deemed to be part thereof, for the purposes of this Treaty, and in time
of war, as in time of peace, shall enjoy complete immunity from attack
or injury by belligerents, and from acts calculated to impair their
usefulness as part of the canal.

Article IV

It is agreed that no change of territorial sovereignty or of the international relations of the country or countries traversed by the before-
mentioned canal shall affect the general principle of neutralization or the
obligation of the High Contracting Parties under the present Treaty.

Article V

The present Treaty shall be ratified by the President of the United
States, by and with the advice and consent of the Senate thereof, and by
His Britannic Majesty; and the ratifications shall be exchanged at
Washington or at London at the earliest possible time within six
months from the date hereof.

In faith whereof the respective Plenipotentiaries have signed this Treaty and thereunto affixed their seals.

Done in duplicate at Washington, the 18th day of November, in the year of Our Lord one thousand nine hundred and one.

JOHN HAY   [SEAL.]

PAUNCEFOTE   [SEAL.]

William M. Malloy, ed., *Treaties, Conventions, International Acts, Protocols and Agreements between the United States of America and Other Powers, 1776–1909* (2 vols., Washington, 1910), I, pp. 782–4

4   Decision of the Alaskan Boundary Tribunal, January 24, 1903

The Alaskan boundary dispute remained a source of potential conflict between the United States and Great Britain. President Roosevelt, believing that the validity of his nation's claim was beyond question, threatened to use force to settle the issue. Canada was equally adamant in support of its claim. Roosevelt finally agreed to arbitration, at the same time intimating that only a decision in favour of the United States would be acceptable. Roosevelt appointed as 'impartial jurists' three ardent supporters of the American position. Canada replied in kind with two advocates of its claim. Great Britain, however, chose Lord Alverstone, the Lord Chief Justice of England, to complete the panel. Alverstone proceeded to vote with the American delegation on all substantive questions. Thus, the dispute was settled – and on Roosevelt's terms.

Decision of the Alaskan Boundary Tribunal under the Treaty of January 24, 1903, between the United States and Great Britain

Whereas by a Convention signed at Washington on the 24th day of January 1903, by Plenipotentiaries of and on behalf of His Majesty the King of the United Kingdom of Great Britain and Ireland and of the British Dominions beyond the Seas, Emperor of India, and of and on behalf of the United States of America, it was agreed that a Tribunal should be appointed to consider and decide the questions hereinafter set forth, such Tribunal to consist of six impartial Jurists of repute, who should consider judicially the questions submitted to them each of whom should first subscribe an oath that he would impartially consider the arguments and evidence presented to the said Tribunal, and would decide thereupon according to his true judgment, and that three members of the said Tribunal should be appointed by His Britannic Majesty and three by the President of the United States:

And whereas it was further agreed by the said Convention that the said Tribunal should consider in the settlement of the said questions submitted to its decision the Treaties respectively concluded between His Britannic Majesty and the Emperor of All the Russias under date of the 28th (16th) February AD 1825 and between the United States of America and the Emperor of all the Russias, concluded under date of the 18th (30th) March AD 1867, and particularly the Articles III, IV and V of the first mentioned Treaty, and should also take into consideration any action of the several Governments or of their respective Representatives, preliminary or subsequent to the conclusion of the said Treaties so far as the same tended to show the original and effective understanding of the parties in respect to the limits of their several territorial jurisdictions under and by virtue of the provisions of the said Treaties.

And whereas it was further agreed by the said Convention, referring to Articles III, IV and V of the said Treaty of 1825, that the said Tribunal should answer and decide the following questions: –

(1) What is intended as the point of commencement of the line?

(2) What channel is the Portland Channel?

(3) What course should the line take from the point of commencement to the entrance to Portland Channel?

(4) To what point on the 56th parallel is the line to be drawn from the head of the Portland Channel, and what course should it follow between these points?

(5) In extending the line of demarcation northward from said point on the parallel of the 56th degree of north latitude, following the crest of the mountains situated parallel to the coast until its intersection with the 141st degree of longitude west of Greenwich, subject to the conditions that if such line should anywhere exceed the distance of 10 marine leagues from the ocean, then the boundary between the British and the Russian territory should be formed by a line parallel to the sinuosities of the coast and distant therefrom not more than 10 marine leagues, was it the intention and meaning of the said Convention of 1825 that there should remain in the exclusive possession of Russia a continuous fringe, or strip, of coast on the mainland not exceeding 10 marine leagues in width, separating the British possessions from the bays, ports, inlets, havens, and waters of the ocean, and extending from the said point on the 56th degree of latitude north to a point where such line of demarcation should intersect the 141st degree of longitude west of the meridian of Greenwich?

(6) If the foregoing question should be answered in the negative and in the event of the summit of such mountains proving to be in places more than 10 marine leagues from the coast should the width of the *lisière*, which was to belong to Russia be measured (i) from the mainland coast of the ocean, strictly so-called along a line perpendicular thereto, or (ii) was it the intention and meaning of the said Convention that where the mainland coast is indented by deep inlets forming part of the territorial waters of Russia, the width of the *lisière* was to be measured (*a*) from the line of the general direction of the mainland coast, or (*b*) from the line separating the waters of the ocean from the territorial waters of Russia, or (*c*) from the heads of the aforesaid inlets?

(7) What, if any exist, are the mountains referred to as situated parallel to the coast, which mountains, when within 10 marine leagues from the coast, are declared to form the eastern boundary?

And whereas His Britannic Majesty duly appointed Richard Everard, Baron Alverstone, G.C.M.G. Lord Chief Justice of England, Sir Louis Amable Jetté K.C.M.G. Lieutenant-Governor of the Province of Quebec, and Allen Bristol Aylesworth one of His Majesty's Counsel, and the President of the United States of America duly appointed the Honourable Elihu Root Secretary of War of the United States, the Honourable Henry Cabot Lodge, Senator of the United States from the State of Massachusetts and the Honourable George Turner of the State of Washington, to be members of the said Tribunal.

Now therefore we the Undersigned having each of us first subscribed an oath as provided by the said Convention and having taken into consideration the matters directed by the said Convention to be considered by us, and having judicially considered the said questions submitted to us, do hereby make Answer and Award as follows: –

In answer to the *first* question

The Tribunal unanimously agrees that the point of commencement of the line is Cape Muzon.

In answer to the *second* question

The Tribunal unanimously agrees that the Portland Channel is the Channel which runs from about 55° 56′ NL and passes to the north of Pearse and Wales Islands.

A majority of the Tribunal that is to say Lord Alverstone Mr Root Mr Lodge and Mr Turner decides that the Portland Channel after passing to the north of Wales Island is the channel between Wales Island and Sitklan Island called Tongass Channel. The Portland Channel above mentioned is marked throughout its length by a dotted red line from the point B to the point marked C on the map signed in duplicate

by the members of the Tribunal at the time of signing their decision.
  In answer to the *third* question
  A majority of the Tribunal that is to say Lord Alverstone Mr Root
Mr Lodge and Mr Turner decides that the course of the line from the
point of commencement to the entrance to Portland Channel is the
line marked A B in red on the aforesaid map.
  In answer to the *fourth* question
  A majority of the Tribunal that is to say Lord Alverstone Mr Root
Mr Lodge and Mr Turner decides that the point to which the line is to
be drawn from the head of the Portland Channel is the point on the 56th
parallel of latitude marked D on the aforesaid map and the course which
the line should follow is drawn from C to D on the aforesaid map.
  In answer to the *fifth* question
  A majority of the Tribunal, that is to say Lord Alverstone Mr Root
Mr Lodge and Mr Turner decides that the answer to the above question
is in the affirmative.
  Question five having been answered in the affirmative question *six*
requires no answer.
  In answer to the *seventh* question
  A majority of the Tribunal that is to say Lord Alverstone, Mr Root,
Mr Lodge and Mr Turner decides that the mountains marked S on the
aforesaid map are the mountains referred to as situated parallel to the
coast on that part of the coast where such mountains marked S are
situated and that between the points marked P (mountain marked
S 8,000) on the north and the point marked T (mountain marked
S 7,950) in the absence of further survey the evidence is not sufficient to
enable the Tribunal to say which are the mountains parallel to the
coast within the meaning of the Treaty.
  In witness whereof we have signed the above written decision upon
the questions submitted to us.
  Signed in duplicate this twentieth day of October 1903.

ALVERSTONE
ELIHU ROOT
HENRY CABOT LODGE
Witness   GEORGE TURNER
  REGINALD TOWER:
                    Secretary.
                    Treaties ... *1776–1909*, ed. Malloy, I, pp. 792–
                    794

5   Theodore Roosevelt to Edward VII on Anglo-American Relations, March 9, 1905

President Roosevelt's personal letter to Edward VII contains a succinct statement of the bases for Anglo-American understanding.

Washington, March 9, 1905

MY DEAR KING EDWARD,

On the eve of the inauguration Sir Mortimer handed me Your Majesty's very kind letter, and the miniature of Hampden, than which I could have appreciated nothing more. White, who will hand you this, has repeated to me your conversation with him. Through him I have ventured to send you some studies of mine in our western history.

I absolutely agree with you as to the importance, not merely to ourselves but to all the free peoples of the civilized world, of a constantly growing friendship and understanding between the english-speaking peoples. One of the gratifying things in what has occurred during the last decade has been the growth in this feeling of good will. All I can do to foster it will be done. I need hardly add that, in order to foster it, we need judgement and moderation no less than the good will itself. The larger interests of the two nations are the same; and the fundamental, underlying traits of their characters are also the same. Over here, our gravest problems are those affecting us within. In matters outside our own borders, we are chiefly concerned, first with what goes on south of us, second with affairs in the orient; and in both cases our interests are identical with yours.

It seems to me that if Russia had been wise she would have made peace before the Japanese took Moukden. If she waits until they are north of Harbin the terms will certainly be worse for her. I had this view unofficially conveyed to the Russian Government some weeks ago; and I think it would have been to their interest if they had then acted upon it. . . .

The Letters of Theodore Roosevelt, ed. Elting E. Morison and John M. Blum (Harvard University Press, 8 vols., 1951–4). The Royal Archives, Windsor Castle, by the gracious permission of Her Majesty

III

THE UNITED STATES AND LATIN AMERICA

1   The Cuban-American Treaty of 1903

The United States lost no time in defining its obligations as a world power in dealing with Latin American nations. This was particularly true with respect to Cuba. By the terms of the Treaty of 1903, Cuba became for all practical purposes an American protectorate.

RELATIONS WITH CUBA

Concluded May 22, 1903; ratification advised by Senate March 22, 1904; ratified by the President June 25, 1904; ratifications exchanged July 1, 1904. Proclaimed July 2, 1904

ARTICLES

I Treaties with foreign powers
II Public debts
III Intervention to maintain independence
IV Acts during military occupation

V Sanitation of cities
VI Island of Pines
VII Coaling stations
VIII Ratification

... The President of the United States of America, Herbert G. Squiers, Envoy Extraordinary and Minister Plenipotentiary at Havana,

And the President of the Republic of Cuba, Carlos de Zaldo y Beurmann, Secretary of State and Justice, – who after communicating to each other their full powers found in good and due form, have agreed upon the following articles:

ARTICLE I

The Government of Cuba shall never enter into any treaty or other compact with any foreign power or powers which will impair or tend to impair the independence of Cuba, nor in any manner authorize or permit any foreign power or powers to obtain by colonization or for military or naval purposes, or otherwise, lodgment in or control over any portion of said island.

Article II

The Government of Cuba shall not assume or contract any public debt to pay the interest upon which, and to make reasonable sinking-fund provision for the ultimate discharge of which, the ordinary revenues of the Island of Cuba, after defraying the current expenses of the Government, shall be inadequate.

Article III

The Government of Cuba consents that the United States may exercise the right to intervene for the preservation of Cuban independence, the maintenance of a government adequate for the protection of life, property, and individual liberty, and for discharging the obligations with respect to Cuba imposed by the Treaty of Paris on the United States, now to be assumed and undertaken by the Government of Cuba.

Article IV

All acts of the United States in Cuba during its military occupancy thereof are ratified and validated, and all lawful rights acquired thereunder shall be maintained and protected.

Article V

The Government of Cuba will execute, and, as far as necessary, extend the plans already devised, or other plans to be mutually agreed upon, for the sanitation of the cities of the island, to the end that a recurrence of epidemic and infectious diseases may be prevented, thereby assuring protection to the people and commerce of Cuba, as well as to the commerce of the Southern ports of the United States and the people residing therein.

Article VI

The Island of Pines shall be omitted from the boundaries of Cuba specified in the Constitution, the title thereto being left to future adjustment by treaty.

ARTICLE VII

To enable the United States to maintain the independence of Cuba, and to protect the people thereof, as well as for its own defense, the Government of Cuba will sell or lease to the United States lands necessary for coaling or naval stations, at certain specified points, to be agreed upon with the President of the United States.

ARTICLE VIII

The present Convention shall be ratified by each party in conformity with the respective Constitutions of the two countries, and the ratifications shall be exchanged in the City of Washington within eight months from this date.

In witness whereof, we the respective Plenipotentiaries, have signed the same in duplicate, in English and Spanish, and have affixed our respective seals at Havana, Cuba, this twenty-second day of May, in the year nineteen hundred and three.

H. G. SQUIERS   [SEAL.]

CARLOS DE ZALDO   [SEAL.]

Treaties . . . *1776–1909*, ed. Malloy, I, 362–4

2.   The Roosevelt Corollary to the Monroe Doctrine, December 6, 1904

President Roosevelt's Annual Message of 1904 was the occasion for a forthright statement of American policy. In order to forestall any possibility of foreign intervention in Latin America, the United States would assume the role of a policeman for that region. This declaration, known as the Roosevelt Corollary to the Monroe Doctrine, stood as the basis for America's relations with its southern neighbours for more than three decades.

. . . In treating of our foreign policy and of the attitude that this great nation should assume in the world at large, it is absolutely necessary to consider the army and the navy, and the Congress, through which the thought of the nation finds its expression, should keep ever vividly in mind the fundamental fact that it is impossible to treat our foreign policy, whether this policy takes shape in the effort to secure justice for others or justice for ourselves, save as conditioned upon the attitude we are willing to take toward our army, and especially toward our navy. It is not merely unwise, it is contemptible, for a nation, as for an individual to use high-sounding language to proclaim its purposes, or to take positions which are ridiculous if unsupported by potential force, and then to refuse to provide this force. If there is no intention of providing and of keeping the force necessary to back up a strong attitude, then it is far better not to assume such an attitude.

The steady aim of this nation, as of all enlightened nations, should be to strive to bring ever nearer the day when there shall prevail throughout the world the peace of justice. There are kinds of peace which are highly undesirable, which are in the long run as destructive as any war. Tyrants and oppressors have many times made a wilderness and called it peace. Many times peoples who were slothful or timid or shortsighted, who had been enervated by ease or by luxury, or misled by false teachings, have shrunk in unmanly fashion from doing duty that was stern and that needed self-sacrifice, and have sought to hide from their own minds their shortcomings, their ignoble motives, by calling them love of peace. The peace of tyrannous terror, the peace of craven weakness, the peace of injustice, all these should be shunned as we shun unrighteous war. The goal to set before us as a nation, the goal which should be set before all mankind, is the attainment of the peace of justice, of the peace which comes when each nation is not merely safeguarded in its own rights, but scrupulously recognizes and performs its duty toward others. Generally peace tells for righteousness; but if there is conflict between the two, then our fealty is due first to the cause of righteousness. Unrighteous wars are common, and unrighteous peace is rare; but both should be shunned. The right of freedom and the responsibility for the exercise of that right cannot be divorced. One of our great poets has well and finely said that freedom is not a gift that tarries long in the hands of cowards. Neither does it tarry long in the hands of those too slothful, too dishonest, or too unintelligent to exercise it. The eternal vigilance which is the price of liberty must be exercised, sometimes to guard against outside foes; although of course far more often to guard against our own selfish or thoughtless shortcomings.

If these self-evident truths are kept before us, and only if they are so kept before us, we shall have a clear idea of what our foreign policy in its larger aspects should be. It is our duty to remember that a nation has no more right to do injustice to another nation, strong or weak, than an individual has to do injustice to another individual; that the same moral law applies in one case as in the other. But we must also remember that it is as much the duty of the nation to guard its own rights and its own interests as it is the duty of the individual so to do. Within the nation the individual has now delegated this right to the State, that is, to the representative of all the individuals, and it is a maxim of the law that for every wrong there is a remedy. But in international law we have not advanced by any means as far as we have advanced in municipal law. There is as yet no judicial way of enforcing a right in international law. When one nation wrongs another or wrongs many others, there is no tribunal before which the wrong-doer can be brought. Either it is necessary supinely to acquiesce in the wrong, and thus put a premium upon brutality and aggression, or else it is necessary for the aggrieved nation valiantly to stand up for its rights. Until some method is devised by which there shall be a degree of international control over offending nations, it would be a wicked thing for the most civilized powers, for those with most sense of international obligations and with keenest and most generous appreciation of the difference between right and wrong, to disarm. If the great civilized nations of the present day should completely disarm, the result would mean an immediate recrudescence of barbarism in one form or another. Under any circumstances a sufficient armament would have to be kept up to serve the purposes of international police; and until international cohesion and the sense of international duties and rights are far more advanced than at present, a nation desirous both of securing respect for itself and of doing good to others must have a force adequate for the work which it feels is allotted to it as its part of the general world duty. Therefore it follows that a self-respecting, just, and far-seeing nation should on the one hand endeavor by every means to aid in the development of the various movements which tend to provide substitutes for war, which tend to render nations in their actions toward one another, and indeed toward their own peoples, more responsive to the general sentiment of humane and civilized mankind; and on the other hand that it should keep prepared while scrupulously avoiding wrong-doing itself, to repel any wrong, and in exceptional cases to take action which in a more advanced stage of international relations would come under the head of the exercise of the international peace. A great free people owes it to itself and to all mankind not to sink into helplessness before the powers of evil.

We are in every way endeavoring to help on, with cordial good-will, every movement which will tend to bring us into more friendly relations with the rest of mankind. In pursuance of this policy I shall shortly lay before the Senate treaties of arbitration with all powers which are willing to enter into these treaties with us. It is not possible at this period of the world's development to agree to arbitrate all matters, but there are many matters of possible difference between us and other nations which can thus be arbitrated. Furthermore, at the request of the Interparliamentary Union, an eminent body composed of practical statesmen from all countries, I have asked the powers to join with this government in a second Hague conference, at which it is hoped that the work already so happily begun at The Hague may be carried some steps further toward completion. This carries out the desire expressed by the first Hague conference itself.

It is not true that the United States feels any land hunger or entertains any projects as regards the other nations of the western hemisphere save such as are for their welfare. All that this country desires is to see the neighbouring countries stable, orderly, and prosperous. Any country whose people conduct themselves well can count upon our hearty friendship. If a nation shows that it knows how to act with reasonable efficiency and decency in social and political matters, if it keeps order and pays its obligations, it need fear no interference from the United States. Chronic wrong-doing, or an impotence which results in a general loosening of the ties of civilized society, may in America, as elsewhere, ultimately require intervention by some civilized nation, and in the western hemisphere the adherence of the United States to the Monroe Doctrine may force the United States, however reluctantly, in flagrant cases of such wrong-doing or impotence, to the exercise of an international police power. If every country washed by the Caribbean Sea would show the progress in stable and just civilization which with the aid of the Platt amendment Cuba has shown since our troops left the island, and which so many of the republics in both Americas are constantly and brilliantly showing, all question of interference by this nation with their affairs would be at an end. Our interests and those of our Southern neighbors are in reality identical. They have great natural riches, and if within their borders the reign of law and justice obtains, prosperity is sure to come to them. While they thus obey the primary laws of civilized society they may rest assured that they will be treated by us in a spirit of cordial and helpful sympathy. We would interfere with them only in the last resort, and then only if it became evident that their inability or unwillingness to do justice at home and abroad had violated the rights of the United States or had invited foreign aggression to the detriment of the entire body of American nations. It is a mere truism to say that every nation, whether in America or anywhere else, which desires to maintain its freedom, its independence, must ultimately realize that the right of such independence cannot be separated from the responsibility of making good use of it.

In asserting the Monroe Doctrine, in taking such steps as we have taken in regard to Cuba, Venezuela, and Panama, and in endeavoring to circumscribe the theatre of war in the Far East, and to secure the open door in China, we have acted in our own interest as well as in the interest of humanity at large. There are, however, cases in which, while our own interests are not greatly involved, strong appeal is made to our sympathies. Ordinarily it is very much wiser and of more useful material betterment to concern ourselves here at home than with trying to better the condition of things in other nations. We have plenty of sins of our own to war against, and under ordinary circumstances we can do more for the general uplifting of humanity by striving with heart and soul to put a stop to civic corruption, to brutal lawlessness and violent race prejudices here at home than by passing resolutions about wrong-doing elsewhere. Nevertheless there are occasional crimes committed on so vast a scale and of such peculiar horror as to make us doubt whether it is not our manifest duty to endeavor at least to show our disapproval of the deed and our sympathy with those who have suffered by it. The cases must be extreme in which such a course is justifiable. There must be no effort made to remove the mote from our brother's eye if we refuse to remove the beam from our own. But in extreme cases action may be justifiable and proper. What form the action shall take must depend upon the circumstances of the case; that is, upon the degree of the atrocity and upon our power to remedy it. The cases in which we could interfere by force of arms as we interfered to put a stop to intolerable conditions in Cuba are necessarily very few. Yet it is not to be expected that a people like ours, which in spite of certain very obvious shortcomings, nevertheless as a whole shows by its consistent practice its belief in the principles of civil and religious liberty and of orderly freedom, a people among whom even the worst crime, like the crime of lynching, is never more than sporadic, so that individuals and not classes are molested in their fundamental rights – it is inevitable that such a nation should desire eagerly to give expression to its horror on an occasion like that of the massacre of the Jews in Kishenef, or when it witnesses such systematic and long extended cruelty and oppression as the cruelty and oppression of which the Armenians have been the victims, and which have won for them the indignant pity of the civilized world. . . .

Fourth Annual Message to Congress, December 6, 1904. *The Works of Theodore Roosevelt*, ed. Hermann Hagedorn (Memorial Edition, 24 vols., New York, 1923–6), xvii, pp. 295–301

3   The Convention of 1907 with the Dominican Republic

The Dominican Republic, debt-ridden and harassed by its European creditors, provided the occasion for a practical application of the Roosevelt Corollary. Under the terms of the Protocol of 1905, the United States assumed responsibility for the collection of Dominican customs and the repayment of foreign debts from this revenue. Although the Senate rejected the Protocol, Roosevelt continued to carry out its terms. The Convention of 1907 formalised this arrangement.

CONVENTION PROVIDING FOR THE ASSISTANCE OF THE UNITED STATES IN THE COLLECTION AND APPLICATION OF THE CUSTOMS REVENUES OF THE DOMINICAN REPUBLIC.

Concluded February 8, 1907; ratification advised by the Senate February 25, 1907; ratified by the President June 22, 1907; ratifications exchanged July 8, 1907; proclaimed July 25, 1907

ARTICLES

I Receiver	IV Accounts of receiver
II Payment of customs revenues	V Ratification
III Public debt	

Whereas during disturbed political conditions in the Dominican Republic debts and claims have been created, some by regular and some by revolutionary governments, many of doubtful validity in whole or in part, and amounting in all to over $30,000,000, nominal or face value;

And whereas the same conditions have prevented the peaceable and continuous collection and application of National revenues for payment of interest or principal of such debts or for liquidation and settlement of such claims; and the said debts and claims continually increase by accretion of interest and are a grievous burden upon the people of the Dominican Republic and a barrier to their improvement and prosperity;

And whereas the Dominican Government has now effected a conditional adjustment and settlement of said debts and claims under which all its foreign creditors have agreed to accept about $12,407,000 for debts and claims amounting to about $21,184,000 of nominal or face value, and the holders of internal debts or claims of about $2,028,258 nominal or face value have agreed to accept about $645,827 therefor, and the remaining holders of internal debts or claims on the same basis as the assents already given will receive about $2,400,000 therefor, which sum the Dominican Government has fixed and determined as the amount which it will pay to such remaining internal debt holders; making the total payments under such adjustment and settlement, including interest as adjusted and claims not yet liquidated, amount to not more than about $17,000,000.

And whereas a part of such plan of settlement is the issue and sale of bonds of the Dominican Republic to the amount of $20,000,000 bearing five per cent interest payable in fifty years and redeemable after ten years at $102\frac{1}{2}$ and requiring payment of at least one per cent per annum for amortization, the proceeds of said bonds, together with such funds as are now deposited for the benefit of creditors from customs revenues of the Dominican Republic heretofore received, after payment of the expenses of such adjustment, to be applied first to the payment of said debts and claims as adjusted and second out of the balance remaining to the retirement and extinction of certain concessions and harbor monopolies which are a burden and hindrance to the commerce of the country and third the entire balance still remaining to the contruction of certain railroads and bridges and other public improvements necessary to the industrial development of the country;

And whereas the whole of said plan is conditioned and dependent upon the assistance of the United States in the collection of customs revenues of the Dominican Republic and the application thereof so far as necessary to the interest upon and the amortization and redemption of said bonds, and the Dominican Republic has requested the United States to give and the United States is willing to give such assistance:

The Dominican Government, represented by its Minister of State for Foreign Relations, Emiliano Tejera, and its Minister of State for Finance and Commerce, Federico Velasquez H., and the United States Government, represented by Thomas C. Dawson, Minister Resident and Consul General of the United States to the Dominican Republic, have agreed:

I That the President of the United States shall appoint, a General Receiver of Dominican Customs, who, with such Assistant Receivers and other employees of the Receivership as shall be appointed by the President of the United States in his discretion, shall collect all the customs duties accruing at the several customs houses of the Dominican Republic until the payment or retirement of any and all bonds issued by the Dominican Government in accordance with the plan and under the limitations as to terms and amounts hereinbefore recited; and said General Receiver shall apply the sums so collected, as follows:

First, to paying the expenses of the receivership; second, to the payment of interest upon said bonds; third, to the payment of the annual sums provided for amortization of said bonds including interest upon all bonds held in sinking fund; fourth, to the purchase and cancellation or the retirement and cancellation pursuant to the terms thereof of any of said bonds as may be directed by the Dominican Government; fifth, the remainder to be paid to the Dominican Government.

The method of distributing the current collections of revenue in order to accomplish the application thereof as hereinbefore provided shall be as follows:

The expenses of the receivership shall be paid by the Receiver as they arise. The allowances to the General Receiver and his assistants for the expenses of collecting the revenues shall not exceed five per cent unless by agreement between the two Governments.

On the first day of each calendar month the sum of $100,000 shall be paid over by the Receiver to the Fiscal Agent of the loan, and the remaining collection of the last preceding month shall be paid over to the Dominican Government, or applied to the sinking fund for the purchase or redemption of bonds, as the Dominican Government shall direct.

Provided, that in case the customs revenues collected by the General Receiver shall in any year exceed the sum of $3,000,000, one half of the surplus above such sum of $3,000,000 shall be applied to the sinking fund for the redemption of bonds.

II The Dominican Government will provide by law for the payment of all customs duties to the General Receiver and his assistants, and will give to them all needful aid and assistance and full protection to the extent of its powers. The Government of the United States will give to the General Receiver and his assistants such protection as it may find to be requisite for the performance of their duties.

III Until the Dominican Republic has paid the whole amount of the bonds of the debt its public debt shall not be increased except by previous agreement between the Dominican Government and the United States. A like agreement shall be necessary to modify the import duties, it being an indispensable condition for the modification of such duties that the Dominican Executive demonstrate and that the President of the United States recognize that, on the basis of exportations and importations to the like amount and the like character during the two years preceding that in which it is desired to make such modification, the total net customs receipts would at such altered rates of duties have been for each of such two years in excess of the sum of $2,000,000 United States gold.

IV   The accounts of the General Receiver shall be rendered monthy to the Contaduria General of the Dominican Republic and to the State Department of the United States and shall be subject to examination and verification by the appropriate officers of the Dominican and the United States Governments.

V   This agreement shall take effect after its approval by the Senate of the United States and the Congress of the Dominican Republic.

Done in four originals, two being in the English language, and two in the Spanish, and the representatives of the high contracting parties signing them in the City of Santo Domingo this 8th day of February, in the year of our Lord 1907.

THOMAS C DAWSON
EMILIANO TEJERA
FEDERICO VELAZQUEZ H.

Treaties . . . 1776–1909, ed. Malloy, I, 418-20

4   President Taft on Dollar Diplomacy, December 3, 1912

The substance of American policy changed little under President Taft, as the United States continued to intervene in Latin American affairs. But there was a shift in emphasis. Taft was more sensitive to economic factors in international affairs. He explained to Congress the purposes of 'Dollar Diplomacy' in a message of December 3, 1912.

. . . . The diplomacy of the present administration has sought to respond to modern ideas of commercial intercourse. This policy has been characterized as substituting dollars for bullets. It is one that appeals alike to idealistic humanitarian sentiments, to the dictates of sound policy and strategy, and to legitimate commercial aims. It is an effort frankly directed to the increase of American trade upon the axiomatic principle that the Government of the United States shall extend all proper support to every legitimate and beneficial American enterprise abroad. How great have been the results of this diplomacy, coupled with the maximum and minimum provision of the tariff law, will be seen by some consideration of the wonderful increase in the export trade of the United States. Because modern diplomacy is commercial, there has been a disposition in some quarters to attribute to it none but materialistic aims. How strikingly erroneous is such an impression may be seen from a study of the results by which the diplomacy of the United States can be judged. . . .

In Central America the aim has been to help such countries as Nicaragua and Honduras to help themselves. They are the immediate beneficiaries. The national benefit to the United States is two-fold. First, it is obvious that the Monroe doctrine is more vital in the neighborhood of the Panama Canal and the zone of the Caribbean than anywhere else. There, too, the maintenance of that doctrine falls most heavily upon the United States. It is therefore essential that the countries within that sphere shall be removed from the jeopardy involved by heavy foreign debt and chaotic national finances and from the ever-present danger of international complications due to disorder at home. Hence the United States has been glad to encourage and support American bankers who were willing to lend a helping hand to the financial rehabilitation of such countries because this financial rehabilitation and the protection of their customhouses from being the prey of would-be dictators would remove at one stroke the menace of foreign creditors and the menace of revolutionary disorder.

The second advantage to the United States is one affecting chiefly all the southern and Gulf ports and the business and industry of the South. The Republics of Central America and the Caribbean possess great natural wealth. They need only a measure of stability and the means of financial regeneration to enter upon an era of peace and prosperity, bringing profit and happiness to themselves and at the same time creating conditions sure to lead to a flourishing interchange of trade with this country.

I wish to call your especial attention to the recent occurrences in Nicaragua, for I believe the terrible events recorded there during the revolution of the past summer – the useless loss of life, the devastation of property, the bombardment of defenseless cities, the killing and wounding of women and children, the torturing of noncombatants to exact contributions, and the suffering of thousands of human beings – might have been averted had the Department of State, through approval of the loan convention by the Senate, been permitted to carry out its now well-developed policy of encouraging the extending of financial aid to weak Central American States with the primary objects of avoiding just such revolutions by assisting those Republics to rehabilitate their finances, to establish their currency on a stable basis, to remove the customhouses from the danger of revolutions by arranging for their secure administration, and to establish reliable banks.

During this last revolution in Nicaragua, the Government of that Republic having admitted its inability to protect American life and property against acts of sheer lawlessness on the part of the malcontents, and having requested this Government to assume that office, it became necessary to land over 2,000 marines and blue-jackets in Nicaragua. Owing to their presence the constituted Government of Nicaragua was free to devote its attention wholly to its internal troubles, and was thus enabled to stamp out the rebellion in a short space of time. When the Red Cross supplies sent to Granada had been exhausted, 8,000 persons having been given food in one day upon the arrival of the American forces, our men supplied other unfortunate, needy Nicaraguans from their own haversacks. I wish to congratulate the officers and men of the United States Navy and Marine Corps who took part in reestablishing order in Nicaragua upon their splendid conduct, and to record with sorrow the death of seven American marines and bluejackets. Since the reestablishment of peace and order, elections have been held amid conditions of quiet and tranquillity. Nearly all the American marines have now been withdrawn. The country should soon be on the road to recovery. The only apparent danger now threatening Nicaragua arises from the shortage of funds. Although American bankers have already rendered assistance, they may naturally be loathe to advance a loan adequate to set the country upon its feet without the support of some such convention as that of June, 1911, upon which the Senate has not yet acted. . . .

> Message of the President of the United States on
> Our Foreign Relations, Communicated to the Two
> Houses of Congress, December 3, 1912 (Wash-
> ington, 1912), pp. 7-8, 10-11

5   President Wilson and 'A New Latin American Policy', October 27, 1913

President Wilson was not over-concerned with advancing his nation's commercial interests in Latin America. He was much more interested in promoting the growth of democratic institutions in the South. Above all, he stated, 'morality and not expediency is the thing that must guide us'. The following is an excerpt from a speech to the Southern Commercial Congress at Mobile, Alabama.

. . . . I come because I want to speak of our present and prospective relations with our neighbors to the south. I deemed it a public duty, as well as a personal pleasure, to be here to express for myself and for the Government I represent the welcome we all feel to those who represent the Latin American States.

The future, ladies and gentlemen, is going to be very different for this hemisphere from the past. These States lying to the south of us, which have always been our neighbors, will now be drawn closer to us by innumerable ties, and, I hope, chief of all, by the tie of a common understanding of each other. Interest does not tie nations together; it sometimes separates them. But sympathy and understanding does unite them, and I believe that by the new route that is just about to be opened, while we physically cut two continents asunder, we spiritually unite them. It is a spiritual union which we seek.

I wonder if you realize, I wonder if your imaginations have been filled with the significance of the tides of commerce. Your governor alluded in very fit and striking terms to the voyage of Columbus, but Columbus took his voyage under compulsion of circumstances. Constantinople had been captured by the Turks and all the routes of trade with the East had been suddenly closed. If there was not a way across the Atlantic to open those routes again, they were closed forever, and Columbus set out not to discover America, for he did not know that it existed, but to discover the eastern shores of Asia. He set sail for Cathay and stumbled upon America. With that change in the outlook of the world, what happened? England, that had been at the back of Europe with an unknown sea behind her, found that all things had turned as if upon a pivot and she was at the front of Europe; and since then all the tides of energy and enterprise that have issued out of Europe have seemed to be turned westward across the Atlantic. But you will notice that they have turned westward chiefly north of the Equator and that it is the northern half of the globe that has seemed to be filled with the media of intercourse and of sympathy and of common understanding.

Do you not see now what is about to happen? These great tides which have been running along parallels of latitude will now swing southward athwart parallels of latitude, and that opening gate at the Isthmus of Panama will open the world to a commerce that she has not known before, a commerce of intelligence, of thought and sympathy between North and South. The Latin American States, which, to their disadvantage, have been off the main lines, will now be on the main lines. I feel that these gentlemen honoring us with their presence to-day will presently find that some part, at any rate, of the center of gravity of the world has shifted. Do you realize that New York, for example, will be nearer the western coast of South America than she is now to the eastern coast of South America? Do you realize that a line drawn northward parallel with the greater part of the western coast of South America will run only about 150 miles west of New York? The great bulk of South America, if you will look at your globes (not at your Mercator's projection), lies eastward of the continent of North America. You will realize that when you realize that the canal will run southeast, not southwest, and that when you get into the Pacific you will be farther east than you were when you left the Gulf of Mexico. These things are significant, therefore, of this, that we are closing one chapter in the history of the world and are opening another, of great, unimaginable significance.

There is one peculiarity about the history of the Latin American States which I am sure they are keenly aware of. You hear of 'concessions' to foreign capitalists in Latin America. You do not hear of concessions to foreign capitalists in the United States. They are not granted concessions. They are invited to make investments. The work is ours, though they are welcome to invest in it. We do not ask them to supply the capital and do the work. It is an invitation, not a privilege; and States that are obliged, because their territory does not lie within the main field of modern enterprise and action, to grant concessions are in this condition, that foreign interests are apt to dominate their domestic affairs, a condition of affairs always dangerous and apt to become intolerable. What these States are going to see, therefore, is an emancipation from the subordination, which has been inevitable, to foreign enterprise and an assertion of the splendid character which, in spite of these difficulties, they have again and again been able to demonstrate. The dignity, the courage, the self-possession, the self-respect of the Latin American States, their achievements in the face of all these adverse circumstances, deserve nothing but the admiration and applause of the world. They have had harder bargains driven with them in the matter of loans than any other peoples in the world. Interest has been exacted of them that was not exacted of anybody else, because the risk was said to be greater; and then securities were taken that destroyed the risk – an admirable arrangement for those who were forcing the terms! I rejoice in nothing so much as in the prospect that they will now be emancipated from these conditions, and we ought to be the first to take part in assisting in that emancipation. I think some of these gentlemen have already had occasion to bear witness that the Department of State in recent months has tried to serve them in that wise. In the future they will draw closer and closer to us because of circumstances of which I wish to speak with moderation and, I hope, without indiscretion.

We must prove ourselves their friends, and champions upon terms of equality and honor. You cannot be friends upon any other terms than upon the terms of equality. You cannot be friends at all except upon the terms of honor. We must show ourselves friends by comprehending their interest whether it squares with our own interest or not. It is a very perilous thing to determine the foreign policy of a nation in the terms of material interest. It not only is unfair to those with whom you are dealing, but it is degrading as regards your own actions.

Comprehension must be the soil in which shall grow all the fruits of friendship, and there is a reason and a compulsion lying behind all this which is dearer than anything else to the thoughtful men of America. I mean the development of constitutional liberty in the world. Human rights, national integrity, and opportunity as against material interests – that, ladies and gentlemen, is the issue which we now have to face. I want to take this occasion to say that the United States will never again seek one additional foot of territory by conquest. She will devote herself to showing that she knows how to make honorable and fruitful use of the territory she has, and she must regard it as one of the duties of friendship to see that from no quarter are material interests made superior to human liberty and national opportunity. I say this, not with a single thought that anyone will gainsay it, but merely to fix in our consciousness what our real relationship with the rest of America is. It is the relationship of a family of mankind devoted to the development of true constitutional liberty. We know that that is the soil of which the best enterprise springs. We know that this is a cause which we are making in common with our neighbors, because we have had to make it for ourselves.

Reference has been made here to-day to some of the national problems which confront us as a Nation. What is at the heart of all our national problems? It is that we have seen the hand of material interest sometimes about to close upon our dearest rights and possessions. We have seen material interests threaten constitutional freedom in the United States. Therefore we will now know how to sympathize with those in the rest of America who have to contend with such powers, not only within their borders but from outside their borders also.

I know what the response of the thought and heart of America will be to the program I have outlined, because America was created to realize a program like that. This is not America because it is rich. This is not America because it has set up for a great population great opportunities of material prosperity. America is a name which sounds in the ears of men everywhere as a synonym with individual opportunity because a synonym of individual liberty. I would rather belong to a poor nation that was free than to a rich nation that had ceased to be in love with liberty. But we shall not be poor if we love liberty, because the nation that loves liberty truly sets every man free to do his best and be his best, and that means the release of all the splendid energies of a great people who think for themselves. A nation of employees cannot be free any more than a nation of employers can be.

In emphasizing the points which must unite us in sympathy and in spiritual interest with the Latin American peoples we are only emphasizing the points of our own life, and we should prove ourselves untrue to our own traditions if we proved ourselves untrue friends to them.

Do not think, therefore, gentlemen, that the questions of the day are mere questions of policy and diplomacy. They are shot through with the principles of life. We dare not turn from the principle that morality and not expediency is the thing that must guide us and that we will never condone iniquity because it is most convenient to do so. It seems to me that this is a day of infinite hope, of confidence in a future greater than the past has been, for I am fain to believe that in spite of all the things that we wish to correct the nineteenth century that now lies behind us has brought us a long stage toward the time when, slowly ascending the tedious climb that leads to the final uplands, we shall get our ultimate view of the duties of mankind. We have breasted a considerable part of that climb and shall presently – it may be in a generation or two – come out upon those great heights where there shines unobstructed the light of the justice of God.

'A New Latin-American Policy: Address Delivered Before the Southern Commercial Congress at Mobile, Alabama, October 27, 1913.' *The Public Papers of Woodrow Wilson: The New Democracy*, ed. Ray Stannard Baker and William E. Dodd (2 vols., New York, 1926), I, pp. 64-9

6   Intervention in Haiti: President Wilson to Robert Lansing, August 4, 1915

The situation in Haiti in 1915 paralleled that of the Dominican Republic a decade earlier. European creditors demanded payment of debts, while Haiti teetered on the brink of political and economic collapse. Wilson refused to intervene for the collection of debts. However, he could not stand aside and watch the island dissolve into chaos. He decided to send American troops for the purpose of restoring order and promoting the growth of a constitutional régime.

These are serious matters, and my own judgment is as much perplexed as yours.

I fear we have not the legal authority to do what we apparently ought to do; and that if we do what is necessary it would constitute a case very much like that of Mr. Roosevelt's action in Santo Domingo, and have very much the same issue.

I suppose there is nothing for it but to take the bull by the horns and restore order. A long programme . . . involves legislation and the cooperation of the Senate in treaty-making, and must therefore await the session of our Congress.

In the meantime this is plain to me:

**(1) We must send to Port au Prince a force sufficient to absolutely control the city not only but also the country immediately about it from which it draws its food. I would be obliged if you would ascertain from the Secretary of the Navy whether he has such a force available that can reach there soon.

(2) We must let the present [Haitian] Congress know that we will protect it but that we will not recognize any action on its part which does not put men in charge of affairs whom we can trust to handle and put an end to revolution.

(3) We must give all who now have authority there or desire to have it or who think they have it or are about to have it to understand that we shall take steps to prevent the payment of debts contracted to finance revolution: in other words, that we consider it our duty to insist on constitutional government there and will, if necessary (that is, if they force us to it as the only way) take charge of elections and see that a real government is erected which we can support. . . .

**This will probably involve making the city authorities virtually subordinate to our commanders. They may hand the city government over to us voluntarily.

State Department Archives

7   President Wilson on 'Our Purposes in Mexico', November 24, 1913

Revolution in Mexico posed comparable difficulties for the Wilson administration. Determined that change should occur only through peaceful and democratic methods, the President exerted the utmost pressure on General Victoriano Huerta's revolutionary régime. Ultimately, Wilson's policy proved successful in removing Huerta from power. In late 1915, a provisional government under Venustiano Carranza took office.

Our Purposes in Mexico

The purpose of the United States is solely and singly to secure peace and order in Central America by seeing to it that the processes of self-government there are not interrupted or set aside.

Usurpations like that of General Huerta menace the peace and development of America as nothing else could. They not only render the development of ordered self-government impossible; they also tend to set law entirely aside, to put the lives and fortunes of citizens and foreigners alike in constant jeopardy, to invalidate contracts and concessions in any way the usurper may devise for his own profit, and to impair both the national credit and all the foundations of business, domestic or foreign.

It is the purpose of the United States, therefore, to discredit and defeat such usurpations whenever they occur. The present policy of the Government of the United States is to isolate General Huerta entirely; to cut him off from foreign sympathy and aid from domestic credit, whether moral or material, and so to force him out.

It hopes and believes that isolation will accomplish this end, and shall await the results without irritation or impatience. If General Huerta does not retire by force of circumstances, it will become the duty of the United States to use less peaceful means to put him out. It will give other governments notice in advance of each affirmative or aggressive step it has in contemplation, should it unhappily become necessary to move actively against the usurper; but no such step seems immediately necessary.

Its fixed resolve is, that no such interruptions of civil order shall be tolerated so far as it is concerned. Each conspicuous instance in which usurpations of this kind are prevented will render their recurrence less likely, and in the end a state of affairs will be secured in Mexico and elsewhere upon this continent which will assure the peace of America and the untrammeled development of its economic and social relations with the rest of the world.

Beyond this fixed purpose the Government of the United States will not go. It will not permit itself to seek any special or exclusive advantages in Mexico or elsewhere for its own citizens, but will seek, here as elsewhere, to show itself the consistent champion of the open door.

In the meantime it is making every effort that the circumstances permit to safeguard foreign lives and property in Mexico and is making the lives and fortunes of the subjects of other governments as much its concern as the lives and fortunes of its own citizens.

> Sent over the signature of the Secretary of State to all embassies except Turkey and Mexico. State Department Archives.

8   President Wilson on Mexico and American Ideals, June 30, 1916

Carranza proved both a patriot and an enlightened leader. But he faced continued difficulties in consolidating his power, particularly from the forces of Pancho Villa in northern Mexico. A strange mixture of patriot and bandit, Villa conducted raids on both sides of the border. In March 1916 he attacked and burned Columbus, New Mexico. The American government, with Carranza's reluctant consent, dispatched an expeditionary force to deal with Villa. As American troops penetrated deeper into Mexico, a series of incidents brought the United States and Mexico to the brink of war. But Wilson, his eye on the situation in Europe, refused to be provoked by either the Mexicans or American public opinion.

I realize that I have done a very impudent thing; I have come to address this thoughtful company of men without any preparation whatever. If I could have written as witty a speech as Mr. Pulitzer, I would have written it. If I could have written as clear an enunciation of the fundamental ideas of American patriotism as the mayor, I should have attempted it. If I could have been as appealing a person and of as feeling a heart as Mr. Cobb, I would have felt safe.

If I could have been as generous and interesting and genuine as Mr. Colby, I should have felt that I could let myself go without any preparation. But, gentlemen, as a matter of fact, I have been absorbed by the responsibilities which have been so frequently referred to here to-night, and that preoccupation has made it impossible for me to forecast even what you would like to hear me talk about.

There is something very oddly contradictory about the effect you men have on me. You are sometimes, particularly in your photographic enterprises, very brutal to me, and you sometimes invade my privacy, even to the extent of formulating my judgments before they are formed, and yet I am tempted when I stand face to face with you to take off all guard and merely expose myself to you as the fallible human being that I am.

Mr. Colby said something that was among the few things I had forecast to say myself. He said that there are some things which it is really useless to debate, because they go as a matter of course.

Of course it is our duty to prepare this Nation to take care of its honor and of its institutions. Why debate any part of that, except the detail, except the plan itself, which is always debatable?

Of course it is the duty of the Government, which it will never overlook, to defend the territory and people of this country. It goes without saying that it is the duty of the administration to have constantly in mind with the utmost sensitiveness every point of national honor.

But, gentlemen, after you have said and accepted these obvious things your program of action is still to be formed. When will you act and how will you act?

The easiest thing is to strike. The brutal thing is the impulsive thing. No man has to think before he takes aggressive action; but before a man really conserves the honor by realizing the ideals of the Nation he has to think exactly what he will do and how he will do it.

Do you think the glory of America would be enhanced by a war of conquest in Mexico? Do you think that any act of violence by a powerful nation like this against a weak and destructive neighbor would reflect distinction upon the annals of the United States?

Do you think that it is our duty to carry self-defense to a point of dictation into the affairs of another people? The ideals of America are written plain upon every page of American history.

And I want you to know how fully I realize whose servant I am. I do not own the Government of the United States, even for the time being. I have no right in the use of it to express my own passions.

I have no right to express my own ambitions for the development of America if those ambitions are not coincident with the ambitions of the Nation itself.

And I have constantly to remind myself that I am not the servant of those who wish to enhance the value of their Mexican investments, that I am the servant of the rank and file of the people of the United States.

I get a great many letters, my fellow citizens, from important and influential men in this country, but I get a great many other letters. I get letters from unknown men, from humble women, from people whose names have never been heard and never will be recorded, and there is but one prayer in all of these letters: 'Mr. President, do not allow anybody to persuade you that the people of this country want war with anybody.'

I got off a train yesterday and as I was bidding goodby to the engineer he said in an undertone, 'Mr. President, keep out of Mexico.' And if one man has said that to me a thousand have said it to me as I have moved about the country.

If I have opportunity to engage them further in conversation, they say, 'Of course, we know that you can not govern the circumstances of the case altogether, and it may be necessary; but for God's sake do not do it unless it is necessary.'

I am for the time being the spokesman of such people, gentlemen. I have not read history without observing that the greatest forces in the world and the only permanent forces are the moral forces.

We have the evidence of a very competent witness, namely, the first Napoleon, who said that as he looked back in the last days of his life upon so much as he knew of human history he had to record the judgment that force had never accomplished anything that was permanent.

Force will not accomplish anything that is permanent, I venture to say, in the great struggle which is going on on the other side of the sea. The permanent things will be accomplished afterwards, when the opinion of mankind is brought to bear upon the issues, and the only thing that will hold the world steady is this same silent, insistent, all-powerful opinion of mankind.

Force can sometimes hold things steady until opinion has time to form, but no force that was ever exerted, except in response to that opinion, was ever a conquering and predominant force.

I think the sentence in American history that I myself am proudest of is that in the introductory sentences of the Declaration of Independence, where the writers say that a due respect for the opinion of mankind demands that they state the reasons for what they are about to do.

I venture to say that a decent respect for the opinions of mankind demanded that those who started the present European war should have stated their reasons; but they did not pay any heed to the opinion of mankind, and the reckoning will come when the settlement comes.

So, gentlemen, I am willing, no matter what my personal fortunes may be, to play for the verdict of mankind. Personally, it will be a matter of indifference to me what the verdict on the 7th of November is, provided I feel any degree of confidence that when a later jury sits I shall get their judgment in my favor. Not my favor personally – what difference does that make? – but in my favor as an honest and conscientious spokesman of a great national convention.

There are some gentlemen who are under the delusion that the power of a nation comes from the top. It does not. It comes from the bottom.

Power and virtue of the tree does not come from the blossoms and fruit down into the roots, but it comes from the roots in the obscure passage of the earth where the power is derived, which displays itself in the blossoms and the fruit; and I know that among the silent, speechless masses of the American people is slowly coming up the sap of moral purpose and love of justice and reverence for humanity which constitutes the only virtue and distinction of the American people.

Look for your rulers of the future! Can you pick out the families that are to produce them? Can you pick out the localities that are going to produce them?

You have heard what has been said about Abraham Lincoln. It is singular how touching every reference to Abraham Lincoln is. It always makes you feel that you wish you had been there to help him in some fashion to fight the battles that he was fighting, sometimes almost alone.

Could you have predicted, if you had seen Abraham Lincoln's birth and boyhood, where that great ruling figure of the world was going to spring from?

I have presided over a university, but I never deceived myself by supposing that by university processes you were producing the ruling forces of the world.

I knew that all a university could do if it knew its business was to interpret the moral forces of the world and let the young man, who sat under its influence, know the very truth of truths about where it came from, and that no man could produce it unless he felt in his blood every corpuscle spring into delightful life with the mention of ideals which have lifted men slowly, oh, so slowly, up the arduous grades, which have resisted the progress since the world began.

So, gentlemen, I have not come here to-night to do anything but to remind that you do not constitute the United States; that I do not constitute the United States; that it is something bigger and greater and finer than any of us; that it was born in an ideal, and only by pursuing an ideal in the face of every adverse circumstance will it continue to deserve the beloved name which we love and for which we are ready to die, the name 'America.'

'We Are the Servants of the Rank and File of the People: Address Before the Press Club, New York, June 30, 1916.' *The Public Papers of Woodrow Wilson: The New Democracy*, ed. Ray Stannard Baker and William E. Dodd (2 vols., New York, 1926), II, pp. 64-9

IV

THE UNITED STATES AND THE FAR EAST

1 The First Open Door Note, September 6, 1899

Secretary Hay, responding to a threatened fragmentation of China into spheres of influence, set forth the principle of equal commercial opportunity for all nations in a circular letter on September 6, 1899. Despite the ambiguous replies of European powers, Hay proclaimed the acceptance of this principle on March 20, 1900.

Mr. Hay to Mr. White

No. 927.]   DEPARTMENT OF STATE,
                                    Washington, September 6, 1899.

SIR:

At the time when the Government of the United States was informed by that of Germany that it had leased from His Majesty the Emperor of China the port of Kiao-chao and the adjacent territory in the province of Shantung, assurances were given to the ambassador of the United States at Berlin by the Imperial German minister for foreign affairs that the rights and privileges insured by treaties with China to citizens of the United States would not thereby suffer or be in anywise impaired within the area over which Germany had thus obtained control.

More recently, however, the British Government recognized by a formal agreement with Germany the exclusive right of the latter country to enjoy in said leased area and the contiguous 'sphere of influence or interest' certain privileges, more especially those relating to railroads and mining enterprises; but as the exact nature and extent of the rights thus recognized have not been clearly defined, it is possible that serious conflicts of interest may at any time arise not only between British and German subjects within said area, but that the interests of our citizens may also be jeopardized thereby.

Earnestly desirous to remove any cause of irritation and to insure at the same time to the commerce of all nations in China the undoubted benefits which should accrue from a formal recognition by the various powers claiming 'spheres of interest' that they shall enjoy perfect equality of treatment for their commerce and navigation within such 'spheres', the Government of the United States would be pleased to see His German Majesty's Government give formal assurances, and lend its cooperation in securing like assurances from the other interested powers, that each, within its respective sphere of whatever influence –

First. Will in no way interfere with any treaty port or any vested interest within any so-called 'sphere of interest' or leased territory it may have in China.

Second. That the Chinese treaty tariff of the time being shall apply to all merchandise landed or shipped to all such ports as are within said 'sphere of interest' (unless they be 'free ports'), no matter to what nationality it may belong, and that duties so leviable shall be collected by the Chinese Government.

Third. That it will levy no higher harbor dues on vessels of another nationality frequenting any port in such 'sphere' than shall be levied on vessels of its own nationality, and no higher railroad charges over lines built, controlled, or operated within its 'sphere' on merchandise belonging to citizens or subjects of other nationalities transported through such 'sphere' than shall be levied on similar merchandise belonging to its own nationals transported over equal distances.

The liberal policy pursued by His Imperial German Majesty in declaring Kiao-chao a free port and in aiding the Chinese Government in the establishment there of a custom-house are so clearly in line with the proposition which this Government is anxious to see recognized that it entertains the strongest hope that Germany will give its acceptance and hearty support.

The recent ukase of His Majesty the Emperor of Russia declaring the port of Ta-lien-wan open during the whole of the lease under which it is held from China to the merchant ships of all nations, coupled with the categorical assurances made to this Government by His Imperial Majesty's representative at this capital at the time and since repeated to me by the present Russian ambassador, seem to insure the support of the Emperor to the proposed measure. Our ambassador at the Court of St. Petersburg has in consequence been instructed to submit it to the Russian Government and to request their early consideration of it. A copy of my instruction on the subject to Mr. Tower is herewith inclosed for your confidential information.

The commercial interests of Great Britain and Japan will be so clearly served by the desired declaration of intentions, and the views of the Governments of these countries as to the desirability of the adoption of measures insuring the benefits of equality of treatment of all foreign trade throughout China are so similar to those entertained by the United States, that their acceptance of the propositions herein outlined and their cooperation in advocating their adoption by the other powers can be confidently expected. I inclose herewith copy of the instruction which I have sent to Mr. Choate on the subject.

In view of the present favorable conditions, you are instructed to submit the above considerations to His Imperial German Majesty's Minister for Foreign Affairs, and to request his early consideration of the subject.

Copy of this instruction is sent to our ambassadors at London and at St. Petersburg for their information.

I have, etc.,   JOHN HAY
Papers Relating to the Foreign Relations of the United States, 1899 (Washington, 1901), pp. 129-30

2   The Second Open Door Note, July 3, 1900

In the midst of the Boxer Rebellion, Secretary Hay added another point to the Open Door. The United States, he announced, was committed to preserving China's territorial and administrative integrity. How the United States intended to implement this objective was – and remained – unclear.

[Circular telegram]

DEPARTMENT OF STATE,
Washington, July 3, 1900.
In this critical posture of affairs in China it is deemed appropriate to define the attitude of the United States as far as present circumstances permit this to be done. We adhere to the policy initiated by us in 1857, of peace with the Chinese nation, of furtherance of lawful commerce, and of protection of lives and property of our citizens by all means guaranteed under extraterritorial treaty rights and by the law of nations. If wrong be done to our citizens we propose to hold the responsible authors to the uttermost accountability. We regard the condition at Pekin as one of virtual anarchy, whereby power and responsibility are practically devolved upon the local provincial authorities. So long as they are not in overt collusion with rebellion and use their power to

protect foreign life and property we regard them as representing the Chinese people, with whom we seek to remain in peace and friendship. The purpose of the President is, as it has been heretofore, to act concurrently with the other powers, first, in opening up communication with Pekin and rescuing the American officials, missionaries, and other Americans who are in danger; secondly, in affording all possible protection everywhere in China to American life and property; thirdly, in guarding and protecting all legitimate American interests; and fourthly, in aiding to prevent a spread of the disorders to the other provinces of the Empire and a recurrence of such disasters. It is, of course, too early to forecast the means of attaining this last result; but the policy of the Government of the United States is to seek a solution which may bring about permanent safety and peace to China, preserve Chinese territorial and administrative entity, protect all rights guaranteed to friendly powers by treaty and international law, and safeguard for the world the principle of equal and impartial trade with all parts of the Chinese Empire.

You will communicate the purport of this instruction to the minister for foreign affairs.

HAY

Papers Relating to the Foreign Relations of the
United States, 1900 (Washington, 1902), p. 299

3   President Roosevelt on 'The Pacific Era', October 1907

President Roosevelt, with characteristic flamboyance, stated the most extreme case for American interest in the Far East. This view, not uncommon at the time, would be echoed by various political and military leaders in the years to come.

Before I visited the Pacific slope I was an expansionist, and since then I have never understood how any man convinced of his country's greatness and glad that his country should challenge with proud confidence its mighty future, can be anything but an expansionist. An ordinary knowledge of the geography of the country should convey, but familiarity with the situation should emphasize, the conviction, that in the century now opening, the commerce and the command of the Pacific will be factors of incalculable moment in the world's history.

The seat of power ever shifts from land to land, from sea to sea. The earliest civilizations, those seated beside the Nile and in Mesopotamia, had little to do with sea traffic. But with the rise of those people who went down to the sea in ships, with the rise of the Phoenicians, the men of Tyre and Sidon, the Mediterranean became the central sea on whose borders lay the great, wealthy and cultivated powers of antiquity. The war navies and the merchant marines of Carthage, Greece and Rome strove thereon for military and industrial supremacy. Its control was the prerequisite to greatness and the Roman became the lord of the Western world only when, after Pompey's naval victories, his fleet rode unchallenged from the Ægean to the Pillars of Hercules. When Rome declined, for centuries thereafter the wealth and culture of Europe were centered on its southern slopes and the control of the Mediterranean was vital in favoring or checking their growth. It was at this time that Venice and Genoa flourished in their grandeur and in their might.

But gradually the nations of the north grew beyond barbarism, and developed fleets and commerce of their own. The North Sea, the Baltic, the Bay of Biscay, saw trading cities rise to become independent or else to become props of mighty civilized nations. The sea-faring merchants ventured with ever greater boldness into the Atlantic. The cities of the Netherlands, the ports of the Hansa, grew and flourished as once the Italian cities had grown. Holland and England, and Spain, Portugal and France sent forth mercantile adventurers to strive for fame and profit on the high seas. The Cape of Good Hope was doubled, America was discovered and the Atlantic ocean became to the greater modern world what the Mediterranean had been to the lesser world of antiquity.

In our own day, the greatest of all oceans, of all the seas, and the last to be used on a large scale by civilized man, bids fair to become in its turn the first in point of importance. The empire that shifted from the Mediterranean will in the life time of those now children bid fair to shift once more westward to the Pacific. When the Nineteenth Century opened, the lonely keels of a few whale ships, a few merchantmen, had begun to furrow the vast expanse of the Pacific; but as a whole its islands and its shores were not materially changed from what they had been in the long past ages when the Phœnician galleys traded in the purple of Tyre, the ivory of Lybia, the treasures of Cyprus. The junks of the Orient still crept between China and Japan and Farther India, and from the woody wilderness which shrouded the western shores of our own continent the red lords of the land looked forth upon a waste of waters which only their own canoes traversed. That was but a century ago; and now at the opening of the Twentieth Century, the change is so vast that it is well nigh impossible for us to estimate its importance. In the South seas the great commonwealth of Australia has sprung into being. Japan, shaking off the lethargy of centuries, has taken her rank among other civilized modern powers. European nations have seated themselves along the eastern coast of Asia; and China now bids fair in her turn to rise and see the industry and aptitude of her teeming population rewarded by national growth.

Meanwhile our own mighty republic has stretched from the Atlantic to the Pacific, and now in California, Oregon and Washington, in Alaska, Hawaii and the Philippines, holds an extent of coast line which makes it of necessity a power of the first class in the Pacific. The extension in the area of our domain has been immense, the extension in the area of our influence even greater. America's geographical position on the Pacific is such as to insure peaceful domination of its waters in the future if we only grasp with sufficient resolution the advantages of that position. We are taking long strides in that direction; witness the cables we are laying down, the steamship lines we are starting – some of them already containing steamships larger than any freight carriers that have previously existed. We have taken the first steps toward digging an Isthmian Canal to be under our own control, a canal which will make our Atlantic and Pacific coast lines in effect continuous, which will be of invaluable benefit to our mercantile navy, and above all to our military navy in the event of war.

The inevitable march of events gave us the control of the Philippine Islands at a time so opportune that it may without irreverence be called Providential. Unless we show ourselves weak, unless we show ourselves degenerate sons of the sires from whose loins we sprung, we must go on with the work we have undertaken. I most earnestly hope that this work will ever be of a peaceful character. We infinitely desire peace and the surest way of obtaining it is to show that we are not afraid of war. We should deal in a spirit of justice and fairness with weaker nations and we should show to the strongest that we are able to maintain our rights. Such showing can not be made by bluster; for bluster merely invites contempt. Let us speak courteously, deal fairly and keep ourselves armed and ready. If we do these things we can count on the peace that comes to the just man armed, to the just man who neither fears nor inflicts wrong. We must keep on building and maintaining a thoroughly efficient navy, with plenty of the best and most formidable ships, with an ample supply of officers and men, and with those officers and men trained in the most efficient fashion to perform their duties. Only thus can we assure our position in the world at large. It behooves men of lofty souls, fit and proud to belong to a mighty nation, to see to it that we keep our position in the world; for our proper place is with the great expanding peoples, with the peoples that dare to be great, that accept with confidence a place of leadership in the world. All our people should take that position but especially the men of the Pacific Slope, for much of our expansion must go through the Golden Gate. And inevitably those who are seated by the Pacific must take the lead in, and must profit by, the growth of American influence along the coasts and among the islands of that mighty ocean, where East and West finally become one.

I believe in the people of the United States with all my heart. I am proud that it has been granted to me to be a citizen in a nation of such glorious opportunities, with the wisdom, the hardihood, and the courage to take advantage of them. We have no choice, we people of the United States, as to whether or not we shall play a great part in the world. That has been determined for us by fate, by the march of events. We have to play that part. All that we can decide is whether we shall play it well or ill. We are not and cannot and never will be one of those nations that can progress from century to century doing little and suffering little, standing aside from the great world currents. We must either succeed greatly or fail greatly. The citizen of a small nation may keep his self respect if that nation plays but a small part in the world, because it is physically impossible for the nation to do otherwise; but the citizen of a great nation which plays a small part should hang his head with shame.

Our place as a nation is and must be with the nations that have left indelibly their impress on the centuries. Men will tell you that the great expanding nations of antiquity have passed away. So they have; and so have all others. Those that did not expand passed away and left not so much as a memory behind them. The Roman expanded, the Roman passed away, but the Roman has left the print of his law, of his language, of his masterful ability in administration, deep in the world's history, deeply imprinted in the character of the races that came after him. I ask that this people rise level to the greatness of its opportunities.

The Mediterranean era declined with the Roman Empire and died with the discovery of America.

The Atlantic era is now at the height of its development and must soon exhaust the resources at its command.

The Pacific era, destined to be the greatest of all, and to bring the whole human race at last into one great comity of nations, is just at the dawn. Man, in his migrations westward, has at last traversed the whole round of the planet, and the sons of the newest West now stand on the Pacific coast of America and touch hands across the greatest of oceans with those ancient races of Asia which have from time immemorial dwelt in their present seats. It is the fate of the American people to be placed at the front in the turmoil that must accompany this new placing of the peoples. I believe the contest will be friendly and peaceful; it surely will be if we keep ourselves so strong that we do not have to fear wrong, and at the same time scrupulously respect the rights and feelings of others. Our aim must be to bring all nations into intimate and brotherly association.

We cannot escape our destiny if we would; we must face the performance of our duties to mankind; all we can decide is whether we shall do these duties well or ill. It depends largely upon the present generation of American citizens to say whether our country shall keep in the van of this glorious work and win the chief triumphs for ourselves; or whether we shall supinely permit others to make the effort, to run the risk and to reap the reward.

The Pacific Era (Detroit), (October 1907), I, pp. 1-4

4 The Taft-Katsura Agreement, July 29, 1905

Roosevelt's grandiose vision of America's role in the Pacific was matched only by the sobriety of his actions. Accepting the fact of Japanese power, he sought an accommodation with the island Empire. He approved wholeheartedly of the Taft-Katsura Agreement. Japan, eager to play the role of policeman in the Pacific, proceeded to declare a protectorate over Korea.

The Secretary of War conferred with the Japanese Premier on July 27, 1905. Two days later he dispatched a lengthy cablegram to Secretary of State Root which was, he said, the 'agreed memorandum of conversation between the Prime Minister and myself'. No actual quotations were given. The substance of the conversation was as follows:

Taft: Certain pro-Russian influences in the United States are spreading the theory that Japanese victory would be a certain prelude to her aggression in the direction of the Philippine Islands. But Japan's only real interest in the Philippines would be to have them governed by a strong and friendly power such as the United States. Japan did not desire to have the islands governed either by natives, unfit for the task, or by some unfriendly European power.

Katsura: This is absolutely correct. Japan had no aggressive designs whatever on the Philippines and the insinuation of a 'Yellow Peril' was only a malicious and clumsy slander circulated to damage Japan. The

fundamental principle of Japan's international policy was the maintenance of peace in the Far East. The best and, in fact, the only means for
accomplishing this was the drafting of an understanding among Japan,
the United States and Great Britain which would uphold the open-door
principle. The prime minister well understood the traditional policy of
the United States in this respect and knew that a formal alliance was out
of the question. But could not an understanding or alliance, in practice,
if not in name, be arrived at? Such an understanding would benefit all
the powers concerned and would preserve the peace.

Taft: It is difficult, indeed impossible, for the President of the United
States to enter even an informal understanding without the consent of
the Senate. But without any agreement at all, the people of the United
States were so fully in accord with the policy of Japan and Great
Britain in the maintenance of Far Eastern peace that appropriate action
by the United States could be counted upon, wherever occasion arose,
just as confidently as if a treaty had been signed.

Katsura: As to the Korean question, Korea was the direct cause of the
war with Russia, so a complete solution was a logical consequence. If
left to herself after the war, Korea would certainly drift back to her
former habit of entering into agreements with other powers and thus
would be renewed the international complications which existed before
the war. Therefore, Japan felt compelled to take some definite step to
end the possibility of Korea lapsing into her former condition. This
would mean another war.

Taft: The observations of the prime minister seem wholly reasonable. The personal view of the secretary of war was that Japan should
establish a suzerainty over Korea. This would require that Korea enter
upon no treaties without the consent of Japan. President Roosevelt
would probably concur in this, although the secretary of war had no
mandate from him. Since he had left the United States, Elihu Root had
been appointed secretary of state.

From Henry F. Pringle, *The Life and Times o,*
William Howard Taft (2 vols., New York,
1939), I, pp. 298–9. Printed by permission of
Farrar, Straus, and Co., publishers

5 The Root-Takahira Agreement, November 30, 1908

The Root-Takahira Agreement complemented the understanding between
Taft and Katsura. In return for a pledge to respect American sovereignty over

the Philippines and to adhere to the Open Door in China, the United States accepted Japan's exclusive interest in Korea and southern Manchuria ('existing *status quo*').

The Secretary of State to the Japanese Ambassador

DEPARTMENT OF STATE,
Washington, November 30, 1908.

EXCELLENCY:

I have the honor to acknowledge the receipt of your note of to-day setting forth the result of the exchange of views between us in our recent interviews defining the understanding of the two Governments in regard to their policy in the region of the Pacific Ocean.

It is a pleasure to inform you that this expression of mutual understanding is welcome to the Government of the United States as appropriate to the happy relations of the two countries and as the occasion for a concise mutual affirmation of that accordant policy respecting the Far East which the two Governments have so frequently delared in the past.

I am happy to be able to confirm to your excellency, on behalf of the United States, the declaration of the two Governments embodied in the following words:

(1) It is the wish of the two Governments to encourage the free and peaceful development of their commerce on the Pacific Ocean.

(2) The policy of both Governments, uninfluenced by any aggressive tendencies, is directed to the maintenance of the existing status quo in the region above mentioned, and to the defense of the principle of equal opportunity for commerce and industry in China.

(3) They are accordingly firmly resolved reciprocally to respect the territorial possessions belonging to each other in said region.

(4) They are also determined to preserve the common interests of all powers in China by supporting by all pacific means at their disposal the independence and integrity of China and the principle of equal opportunity for commerce and industry of all nations in that Empire.

(5) Should any event occur threatening the status quo as above described or the principle of equal opportunity as above defined, it remains for the two Governments to communicate with each other in order to arrive at an understanding as to what measures they may consider it useful to take.

Accept, Excellency, the renewed assurance of my highest consideration.

ELIHU ROOT
Papers Relating to the Foreign Relations of the
United States, 1908 (Washington, 1912), pp.
511-12

6   Secretary Knox on the Neutralization of Railroads in Manchuria, January 6, 1910

During the Taft administration, the emphasis of the Open Door shifted from
competition to co-operation. Secretary Knox explained the necessity for this
new policy in a public statement of January 1910.

Statement given to the press

DEPARTMENT OF STATE,
Washington, January 6, 1910.

In reply to an inquiry as to the truth of the St. Petersburg report
relating to the neutralisation of Railways in Manchuria, the Secretary
of State to-day said :

The proposition of the United States to the interested powers looking
to the neutralization of the Manchurian railroads discloses the end
toward which American policy in the Far East has been recently directed.

Late in May last this Government learned that an understanding had
been reached between important British, French, and German financial
groups, supported by their Governments, by which they were to
furnish funds for the construction of two great railways in China. This
Government, believing that sympathetic cooperation between the
Governments most vitally interested would best subserve the policies of
maintenance of Chinese political integrity and equality of commercial
opportunity, suggested that American cooperation with the powerful
international financial group already formed would be useful to further
the policies to which all were alike pledged.

This Government pointed out that the greatest danger at present in
China to the open door and the development of foreign trade arose
from disagreements among the great western nations, and expressed the
opinion that nothing would afford so impressive an object lesson to
China and the world as the sight of the four great capitalist nations –
Great Britain, Germany, France, and the United States – standing
together for equality of commercial opportunity.

Owing to the strong opposition that had developed in certain official quarters in China and elsewhere, the President, in July last, felt warranted in resorting to the somewhat unusual method of communicating directly with His Imperial Highness Prince Chun, regent of the Chinese Empire, informing the latter that he was greatly disturbed at the reports of certain prejudiced opposition to the Chinese Government's arranging for equal participation by American capital in the Hukuang loan. The President pointed out that the wishes of the United States were based upon broad national and impersonal principles of equity and good policy, in which a due regard for the best interests of China had a prominent part. He reasserted his intense personal interest in making the use of American capital in the development of China an instrument in the promotion of China's welfare and an increase in her material prosperity without entanglements or embarrassments that might affect the growth of her independent political power and the preservation of her territorial integrity.

As a result of this communication, an agreement was soon reached with the Chinese Government that American bankers should take one-fourth of the total loan and that Americans and American materials should have all the same rights, privileges, preferences, and discretions for all present and prospective lines that were reserved to the British, German, and French nationals and materials under the terms of their original agreement, except only the right to appoint chief engineers for the two sections about to be placed under contract. As to the latter point, China gave assurance that American engineers would be employed upon the engineering corps of both roads and that the present waiving of America's right to chief engineers would in no way prejudice its rights in that regard when future extensions should be constructed. After several months of continuous negotiation, the right to such American all-round equal participation has been acknowledged and a final settlement on this basis has been all but completed.

The grounds for this energetic action on the part of the United States Government have not been generally understood. Railroad loans floated by China have in the past generally been given an imperial guaranty and secured by first mortgages on the lines constructed or by pledging provincial revenues as security. The proposed hypothecation of China's internal revenues for a loan was therefore regarded as involving important political considerations. The fact that the loan was to carry an imperial guaranty and be secured on the internal revenues made it of the greatest importance that the United States should participate therein in order that this Government might be in a position as an interested party to exercise an influence equal to that of any of the other three powers in any question arising through the pledging of China's national resources, and to enable the United States, moreover, at the proper time again to support China in urgent and desirable fiscal administrative reforms, such as the abolition of likin, the revision of the customs tariff, and general fiscal and monetary rehabilitation.

There were, however, stronger reasons and broader grounds. In fact, the action of the Government in respect to the pending loan was but the first step in a new phase of the traditional policy of the United States in China and with special reference to Manchuria. As is well known, the essential principles of the Hay policy of the open door are the preservation of the territorial and jurisdictional integrity of the Chinese Empire and equal commercial opportunity in China for all nations. This Government believes that one of the most effective, if not the most effective, way to secure for China the undisturbed enjoyment of all political rights in Manchuria and to promote the normal development of the eastern provinces under the policy of the open door practically applied would be to take the railroads of Manchuria out of eastern politics and place them under an economic and impartial administration by vesting in China the ownership of its railroads; the funds for that purpose to be furnished by the nationals of such interested powers as might be willing to participate and who are pledged to the policy of the open door and equal opportunity, the powers participating to operate the railway system during the period of the loan and enjoy the usual preferences in supplying materials.

Such a policy would naturally require for its execution the cooperation not only of China, but also of Japan and of Russia, who already have extensive railway rights in Manchuria. The advantages of such a plan are obvious. It would insure unimpaired Chinese sovereignty, the commercial and industrial development of the Manchurian provinces, and furnish a substantial reason for the early solution of the problems of fiscal and monetary reform which are now receiving such earnest attention by the Chinese Government. It would afford an opportunity for both Russia and Japan to shift their onerous duties, responsibilities, and expenses in connection with these railways to the shoulders of the combined powers, including themselves. Such a policy, moreover, would effect a complete commercial neutralization of Manchuria, and in so doing make a large contribution to the peace of the world by converting the provinces of Manchuria into an immense commercial neutral zone.

The recent signature of an ad referendum agreement between a

representative of the Chinese Government and the financial representatives of the United States and Great Britain to finance and construct a
railway line from Chinchow to Aigun gave the United States an opportunity to lay this proposal before the Government of Great Britain for
its consideration, and it is gratifying to be able to state that the project
has already received the approval in principle of that Government.
There are reasons to believe that such a plan might also meet with like
favorable consideration on the part of Russia. Germany and China
cordially approve the American suggestion, and certain press reports
from Japan indicate that the project may likewise be received with
favor by that country. For instance, a recent article on the subject in the
Japan Mail ends with these significant words:

'One can not conceal from oneself the fact that if all the railways
forming part of the system which connects the west with the Far East
were coverted into a neutral estate a great contribution will be made to
the peace of the world.'

> *Papers Relating to the Foreign Relations of the*
> *United States, 1910* (Washington, 1915), pp.
> 243–5

7   President Wilson on the Open Door, March 19, 1913

The United States returned to the traditional concept of the Open Door in 1913.
Wilson, like his predecessors, desired 'the most extended and intimate trade
relationship' with China, but he refused to become involved in Chinese internal
affairs.

> *The Acting Secretary of State to Certain American Diplomatic*
> *Officers*

[Telegram]

DEPARTMENT OF STATE,
Washington, March 19, 1913 – 9 p.m.

Only for your information and guidance, I quote the following
statement issued by the President:

'We are informed that at the request of the last administration a
certain group of American bankers undertook to participate in the
loan now desired by the Government of China (approximately

$125,000,000). Our Government wished American bankers to participate along with the bankers of other nations, because it desired that the good will of the United States toward China should be exhibited in this practical way, that American capital should have access to that great country, and that the United States should be in a position to share with the other powers any political responsibilities that might be associated with the development of the foreign relations of China in connection with her industrial and commercial enterprises. The present administration has been asked by this group of bankers whether it would also request them to participate in the loan. The representatives of the bankers through whom the administration was approached declared that they would continue to seek their share of the loan under the proposed agreements only if expressly requested to do so by the Government. The administration has declined to make such request, because it did not approve the conditions of the loan or the implications of responsibility on its own part which it was plainly told would be involved in the request.

'The conditions of the loan seem to us to touch very nearly the administrative independence of China itself, and this administration does not feel that it ought, even by implication, to be a party to those conditions. The responsibility on its part which would be implied in requesting the bankers to undertake the loan might conceivably go to length in some unhappy contingency of forcible interference in the financial, and even the political, affairs of that great oriental State, just now awakening to a consciousness of its power and of its obligations to its people. The conditions include not only the pledging of particular taxes, some of them antiquated and burdensome, to secure the loan, but also the administration of those taxes by foreign agents. The responsibility on the part of our Government implied in the encouragement of a loan thus secured and administered is plain enough and is obnoxious to the principles upon which the government of our people rests.

'The Government of the United States is not only willing, but earnestly desirous, of aiding the great Chinese people in every way that is consistent with their untrammeled development and its own immemorial principles. The awakening of the people of China to a consciousness of their responsibilities under free government is the most significant, if not the most momentous, event of our generation. With this movement and aspiration the American people are in profound sympathy. They certainly wish to participate, and participate very generously, in the opening to the Chinese and to the use of the world the almost untouched and perhaps unrivaled resources of China.

'The Government of the United States is earnestly desirous of promoting the most extended and intimate trade relationship between this country and the Chinese Republic. The present administration will urge and support the legislative measures necessary to give American merchants, manufacturers, contractors, and engineers the banking and other financial facilities which they now lack and without which they are at a serious disadvantage as compared with their industrial and commercial rivals. This is its duty. This is the main material interest of its citizens in the development of China. Our interests are those of the open door – a door of friendship and mutual advantage. This is the only door we care to enter.'

ADEE

Papers Relating to the Foreign Relations of the United States, 1913 (Washington, 1920), pp. 170-1

8 Secretary Bryan and the Twenty-One Demands Crisis, May 11, 1915

Japan's twenty-one 'demands' on China in 1915 represented a clear violation of the Open Door. The United States responded to this challenge by applying strong diplomatic and moral pressure on Japan. The following note drew the line sternly.

The Secretary of State to Ambassador Guthrie

[Telegram]

DEPARTMENT OF STATE,
Washington, May 11, 1915 – 5 p.m.

Please call upon the Minister for Foreign Affairs and present to him a note textually as follows:

'In view of the circumstances of the negotiations which have taken place and which are now pending between the Government of Japan and the Government of China, and of the agreements which have been reached as a result thereof, the Government of the United States has the honor to notify the Imperial Japanese Government that it cannot recognize any agreement or undertaking which has been entered into or which may be entered into between the Governments of Japan and China, impairing the treaty rights of the United States and its citizens in China, the political or territorial integrity of the Republic of China,

or the international policy relative to China commonly known as the open door policy.
'An identical note has been transmitted to the Government of the Chinese Republic.'

BRYAN
Papers Relating to the Foreign Relations of the United States, 1915 (Washington, 1924), p. 146

9 The Lansing-Ishii Agreement, November 2, 1917

Once the attention of the western powers was absorbed by the war in Europe, Japan proceeded to consolidate its position in Manchuria and to seize the German concession in Shantung Province. Wilson, like Roosevelt, attempted to deal realistically with growing Japanese power. The Lansing-Ishii Agreement, however, produced only misunderstanding and confusion. The United States interpreted the document as a recognition of Japan's predominant *economic* position on the Asian mainland. Japan viewed the agreement as sanctioning its *political* position.

AGREEMENT EFFECTED BY EXCHANGE OF NOTES BETWEEN THE UNITED STATES AND JAPAN

MUTUAL INTEREST RELATING TO THE REPUBLIC OF CHINA

The Secretary of State to the Japanese Ambassador on Special Mission
DEPARTMENT OF STATE,
Washington, November 2, 1917.

EXCELLENCY:

I have the honor to communicate herein my understanding of the agreement reached by us in our recent conversations touching the questions of mutual interest to our Governments relating to the Republic of China.

In order to silence mischievous reports that have from time to time been circulated, it is believed by us that a public announcement once more of the desires and intentions shared by our two Governments with regard to China is advisable.

The Governments of the United States and Japan recognize that territorial propinquity creates special relations between countries, and, consequently, the Government of the United States recognizes that Japan has special interests in China, particularly in the part to which her possessions are contiguous.

The territorial sovereignty of China, nevertheless, remains unimpaired and the Government of the United States has every confidence in the repeated assurances of the Imperial Japanese Government that while geographical position gives Japan such special interests they have no desire to discriminate against the trade of other nations or to disregard the commercial rights heretofore granted by China in treaties with other powers.

The Governments of the United States and Japan deny that they have any purpose to infringe in any way the independence or territorial integrity of China and they declare, furthermore, that they always adhere to the principle of the so-called 'open door' or equal opportunity for commerce and industry in China.

Moreover, they mutually declare that they are opposed to the acquisition by any Government of any special rights or privileges that would affect the independence or territorial integrity of China or that would deny to the subjects or citizens of any country the full enjoyment of equal opportunity in the commerce and industry of China.

I shall be glad to have your excellency confirm this understanding of the agreement reached by us.

Accept [etc.]

ROBERT LANSING

Protocol

'In the course of the conversations between the Japanese Special Ambassador and the Secretary of State of the United States which have led to the exchange of notes between them dated this day, declaring the policy of the two Governments with regard to China, the question of embodying the following clause in such declaration came up for discussion: "they (the Governments of Japan and the United States) will not take advantage of the present conditions to seek special rights or privileges in China which would abridge the rights of the subjects or citizens of other friendly states."

'Upon careful examination of the question, it was agreed that the clause above quoted being superfluous in the relations of the two Governments and liable to create erroneous impression in the minds of the public, should be eliminated from the declaration.

'It was, however, well understood that the principle enunciated in the clause which was thus suppressed was in perfect accord with the declared policy of the two Governments in regard to China.'

Papers Relating to the Foreign Relations of the United States, 1917 (Washington, 1926), p. 264; *Foreign Relations of the United States, 1922* (2 vols., Washington, 1938), II, p. 595

10   Minister Reinsch's Farewell Message, June 7, 1919

Bitterness and discouragement characterised Minister Paul S. Reinsch's tour of duty in China from 1913 to 1919. American policy in the Far East when viewed from the perspective of Peking gave him little cause for optimism. Reinsch's sentiments would be echoed by many of his successors in the years to come.

June 7, 1919

DEAR MR. PRESIDENT:

I have the honour to place in your hands my resignation as minister to China and to request that I may be relieved of the duties of this post as soon as convenient to yourself and to the Secretary of State. My reason for this action is that I am wearied after nearly six years of continuous strain, that I feel that the interests of my family demand my return to the United States, and that I should like to reënter affairs at home without making my absence so long as to break off all of the most important relationships.

I desire to thank you for the confidence you have reposed in me, and it shall be my greatest desire to continue in the future to coöperate in helping to realize those great purposes of national and international policy which you have so clearly and strongly put before the American nation and the world.

In making this communication to you I cannot but refer to recent developments with respect to China. The general outlook is indeed most discouraging, and it seems impossible to accomplish anything here at present or until the home governments are willing to face the situation and to act. It is not difficulties that deter me, and I should stay at my post if it were necessary and if I did not think that I could be of more use in the United States than in China at the present time. But in fact, the situation requires that the American people should be made to realize what is at stake here for us in order that they may give the necessary backing to the Government for support in any action which the developments here may require. Unless the American people realize this and the Government feels strong enough to take adequate action, the fruits of one hundred and forty years of American work in China will inevitably be lost. Our people will be permitted to exist here only on the sufferance of others, and the great opportunity which has been held out to us by the Chinese people to assist in the development of education and free institutions will be gone beyond recall. In its stead there will come a sinister situation dominated by the unscrupulous methods of the reactionary military régime centred in Tokyo, absolutist in tendency, cynical of the principles of free government and human progress. If this force, with all the methods it is accustomed to apply, remains unopposed there will be created in the Far East the greatest engine of military oppression and dominance that the world has yet seen. Nor can we avoid the conclusion that the brunt of evil results will fall on the United States, as is already foreshadowed by the bitter hostility and abnormal vituperativeness of the Japanese press with regard to America.

The United States and Great Britain will have to stand together in this matter; I do not think this is realized as fully by Britishers at home as by those out here. If Russia can become an independent representative government its interests would parallel ours. The forces of public opinion and strength which can thus be mobilized are entirely sufficient to control the situation here and to keep it from assuming the menacing character which is threatened at present; but this can only be done if the situation is clearly seen and if it is realized that the military part of Japan will continue its present methods and purposes which have proved so successful until it becomes a dead wall of firm, quiet opposition. There will be a great deal of talk of friendship for China, of restoration of Shantung, of loyalty to the League of Nations, but it will be dangerous to accept this and to stop questioning what are the methods actually applied; as long as they exist the menace is growing all the time. We cannot rest secure on treaties nor even on the League of Nations without this checking up of the facts. Otherwise these instruments would only make the game a little more complicated but not change its essential character. The menace can be avoided only if it is made plain to Japan that her purposes are unmistakable and that the methods utilized to effect them will by no means be tolerated. Such purposes are the stirring up of trouble and revolution, encouragement of bandits and pirates, morphia, financial corruption, misleading of the press, refusal of just satisfaction when Americans are injured in order to gain prestige for absolute power, and chief of all official duplicity, such as the disavowal of knowledge when loans are being made to the Chinese Government by leading Japanese banks and the subsequent statement by the Japanese minister that these loans were private arrangements by 'merchants.'

If continuous support could be given not only to the activities of American merchants but to the constructive forces in Chinese national life itself these purposes and methods would not have the chance to flourish and succeed which they now enjoy.

During the war our action in the support of constructive forces in China necessarily could not be effective, as our energies were required elsewhere. Yet I believe that a great opportunity was missed when China had broken off relations with Germany. The very least recognition of her sentiments, support and efforts, on our part, would have changed the entire situation. But while millions upon millions were paid to the least important of the countries of Europe not a cent was forthcoming for China. This lack of support drove Tuan and his followers into the arms of the pro-Japanese agents. Instead of support we gave China the Lansing-Ishii Note.

Throughout this period the Japanese game has still been in the stage of bluff; while Germany seemed at her strongest in the war indeed the Japanese were perhaps making their veiled threats with a feeling that if they should ally themselves with a strong Germany the two would be invincible; but even at that time a portion of the American navy detached could have checkmated Japan. Since the complete breakdown of Germany the case of Japan has been carried through solely on bluff though perhaps it may be that the Japanese militarists have succeeded in convincing themselves that their establishment is formidable. But it is plain that they would be absolutely powerless in the face of a stoppage of commerce and a navy demonstration on the part of any one of the great powers. No one desires to think of this contingency, but it is plain that after the breakdown of Germany it was not feasible for Japan to use force nor could she have suffered a greater damage than to exclude herself from the Peace Conference where she had everything to gain and nothing to lose. In ten years there may be a very different situation. Then also our people, having grown wise, will be sure to shout: 'Why was not this stopped while there was yet time?' It seems to me necessary that someone in the Government ought to give attention primarily to China and the Far Eastern situation. It is very difficult to get any attention for China. I mean any continuous attention that results in getting something actually done. Everything else seems to come first because Europe seems so much nearer; and yet the destinies of Serbia, Czecho-Slovakia, and Greece are infinitesimal in their importance to the future of America compared with those of China.

During my service here I have constantly suffered from this lack of continuous attention at home to the Far Eastern situation. It has reacted on the consular service; the interpreter service which is absolutely necessary to make our consular corps in China effective has been starved, as no new appointments have been made. In my own case promises of assistance which had been given repeatedly went unfulfilled. In this matter I have not the least personal feeling. I know the result is not due to the personal neglect or ill-will of any man or group of men, only it seems to me to indicate a general sentiment of the unimportance of Far Eastern affairs, which ought to be remedied. I repeat that these statements are not made in a spirit of complaint; all individual members of the Department of State have shown nothing but consideration and readiness to assist, but there has been lacking a concentrated interest in China, which ought to be represented in some one of the high officials, designated to follow up Far Eastern affairs and accorded influence commensurate with responsibilities in this matter.

From Paul S. Reinsch, *An American Diplomat in China* (Garden City, New York, 1922), pp. 364-7. Printed by permission of Doubleday & Co., publishers

V

THE UNITED STATES AND THE GREAT WAR: THE DEFENCE OF NEUTRAL RIGHTS

1   President Wilson appeals for Neutrality, August 19, 1914

President Wilson proclaimed American neutrality at the outbreak of the war in Europe. The United States, he believed, could best serve its own interests, as well as the interests of the rest of the world, by remaining aloof from the struggle. In the following statement, the President called for neutrality in thought as well as deed.

MY FELLOW COUNTRYMEN:

I suppose that every thoughtful man in America has asked himself, during these last troubled weeks, what influence the European war may exert upon the United States, and I take the liberty of addressing a few words to you in order to point out that it is entirely within our own choice what its effects upon us will be and to urge very earnestly upon you the sort of speech and conduct which will best safeguard the Nation against distress and disaster.

The effect of the war upon the United States will depend upon what American citizens say and do. Every man who really loves America will act and speak in the true spirit of neutrality, which is the spirit of impartiality and fairness and friendliness to all concerned. The spirit of the Nation in this critical matter will be determined largely by what individuals and society and those gathered in public meetings do and say, upon what newspapers and magazines contain, upon what ministers utter in their pulpits, and men proclaim as their opinions on the street.

The people of the United States are drawn from many nations, and chiefly from the nations now at war. It is natural and inevitable that there should be the utmost variety of sympathy and desire among them with regard to the issues and circumstances of the conflict. Some will wish one nation, others another, to succeed in the momentous struggle. It will be easy to excite passion and difficult to allay it. Those responsible for exciting it will assume a heavy responsibility, responsibility for no less a thing than that the people of the United States, whose love of their country and whose loyalty to its Government should unite them as Americans all, bound in honor and affection to think first of her and her interests, may be divided in camps of hostile opinion, hot against each other, involved in the war itself in impulse and opinion if not in action.

Such divisions amongst us would be fatal to our peace of mind and might seriously stand in the way of the proper performance of our duty as the one great nation at peace, the one people holding itself ready to play a part of impartial mediation and speak the counsels of peace and accommodation, not as a partisan, but as a friend.

I venture, therefore, my fellow countrymen, to speak a solemn word of warning to you against that deepest, most subtle, most essential breach of neutrality which may spring out of partisanship, out of passionately taking sides. The United States must be neutral in fact as well as in name during these days that are to try men's souls. We must be impartial in thought as well as in action, must put a curb upon our sentiments as well as upon every transaction that might be construed as a preference of one party to the struggle before another.

My thought is of America. I am speaking, I feel sure, the earnest wish and purpose of every thoughtful American that this great country of ours, which is, of course, the first in our thoughts and in our hearts, should show herself in this time of peculiar trial a Nation fit beyond others to exhibit the fine poise of undisturbed judgment, the dignity of self-control, the efficiency of dispassionate action; a Nation that neither sits in judgment upon others nor is disturbed in her own counsels and which keeps herself fit and free to do what is honest and disinterested and truly serviceable for the peace of the world.

Shall we not resolve to put upon ourselves the restraints which will bring to our people the happiness and the great and lasting influence for peace we covet for them?

'American Neutrality – An Appeal by the President, August 19, 1914.' *The Public Papers of Woodrow Wilson: The New Democracy*, ed. Ray Stannard Baker and William E. Dodd (2 vols., New York, 1926), I, pp. 64–9

2 Secretary Lansing's Note to Great Britain on Neutral Rights, October 21, 1915

Determined to stand apart from the war, the United States was equally adamant in asserting the rights of a neutral on the high seas. There followed a lengthy quarrel with London over the legality of certain British maritime procedures.

... (33) I believe it has been conclusively shown that the methods sought to be employed by Great Britain to obtain and use evidence of enemy destination of cargoes bound for neutral ports, and to impose a contraband character upon such cargoes, are without justification; that the blockade, upon which such methods are partly founded, is ineffective, illegal, and indefensible; that the judicial procedure offered as a means of reparation for an international injury is inherently defective for the purpose; and that in many cases jurisdiction is asserted in violation of the law of nations. The United States, therefore, can not submit to the curtailment of its neutral rights by these measures, which are admittedly retaliatory, and therefore illegal, in conception and in nature, and intended to punish the enemies of Great Britain for alleged illegalities on their part. The United States might not be in a position to object to them if its interests and the interests of all neutrals were unaffected by them, but, being affected, it can not with complacence suffer further subordination of its rights and interests to the plea that the exceptional geographic position of the enemies of Great Britain require or justify oppressive and illegal practices.

(34) The Government of the United States desires, therefore, to impress most earnestly upon His Majesty's Government that it must insist that the relations between it and His Majesty's Government be governed, not by a policy of expediency, but by those established rules of international conduct upon which Great Britain in the past has held the United States to account when the latter nation was a belligerent engaged in a struggle for national existence. It is of the highest importance to neutrals, not only of the present day, but of the future, that the principles of international right be maintained unimpaired.

(35) This task of championing the integrity of neutral rights, which have received the sanction of the civilized world, against the lawless conduct of belligerents arising out of the bitterness of the great conflict which is now wasting the countries of Europe, the United States unhesitatingly assumes, and to the accomplishment of that task it will devote its energies, exercising always that impartiality which from the

outbreak of the war it has sought to exercise in its relations with the warring nations. . . .

Papers Relating to the Foreign Relations of the United States, 1915, Supplement (Washington, 1928), p. 589

3   Protest to Great Britain against the 'Blacklist', July 26, 1916

The great crisis in Anglo-American relations occurred in the summer of 1916. While definitions of contraband could be argued, blacklisting and the seizure of American mails were viewed as direct affronts to American sovereignty. That Wilson would have taken the United States to war with Britain is doubtful, but a break in diplomatic relations and severe trade restrictions were possibilities. The British, in the end, were able to avoid a direct confrontation only because of the threat to the United States of war with Germany over unrestricted submarine warfare.

The Acting Secretary of State to the Ambassador in Great Britain (Page)

[Telegram]

Washington, July 26, 1916, 10 p.m.

3578. You are instructed to deliver to Grey a formal note on the subject of the enemy-trading act, textually as follows:

The announcement that His Britannic Majesty's Government has placed the names of certain persons, firms, and corporations in the United States upon a proscriptive 'black list', and has forbidden all financial or commercial dealings between them and citizens of Great Britain, has been received with the most painful surprise by the people and Government of the United States, and seems to the Government of the United States to embody a policy of arbitrary interference with neutral trade against which it is its duty to protest in the most decided terms.

The scope and effect of the policy are extraordinary. British steamship companies will not accept cargoes from the proscribed firms or persons or transport their goods to any port, and steamship lines under neutral ownership understand that if they accept freight from them they are likely to be denied coal at British ports and excluded from other privileges which they have usually enjoyed and may themselves be put upon the black list. Neutral bankers refuse loans to those on the list and neutral merchants decline to contract for their goods, fearing a like proscription. It appears that British officials regard the prohibitions of the black list as applicable to domestic commercial transactions in foreign countries as well as in Great Britain and her dependencies, for Americans doing business in foreign countries have been put on notice that their dealings with blacklisted firms are to be regarded as subject to veto by the British Government. By the same principle, Americans in the United States might be made subject to similar punitive action if they were found dealing with any of their own countrymen whose names had thus been listed.

The harsh and even disastrous effects of this policy upon the trade of the United States, and upon the neutral rights upon which it will not fail to insist, are obvious. Upon the list of those proscribed and in effect shut out from the general commerce of the world may be found American concerns which are engaged in large commercial operations as importers of foreign products and materials and as distributors of American products and manufacturers to foreign countries, and which constitute important channels through which American trade reaches the outside world. Their foreign affiliations may have been fostered for many years, and when once broken cannot easily or promptly be reestablished. Other concerns may be put upon the list at any time and without notice. It is understood that additions to the proscription may be made 'whenever on account of enemy nationality or enemy association of such persons or bodies of persons it appears to His Majesty expedient to do so'. The possibilities of undeserved injury to American citizens from such measures, arbitrarily taken, and of serious and incalculable interruptions of American trade are without limit.

It has been stated on behalf of His Majesty's Government that these measures were aimed only at the enemies of Great Britain and would be adopted and enforced with strict regard to the rights of neutrals and with the least possible detriment to neutral trade, but it is evident that they are inevitably and essentially inconsistent with the rights of the citizens of all the nations not involved in war. The Government of the United States begs to remind the Government of His Britannic Majesty that citizens of the United States are entirely within their rights in attempting to trade with the people or the governments of any of the nations now at war, subject only to well-defined international practices and understandings which the Government of the United States deems the Government of Great Britain to have too lightly and too frequently disregarded.

There are well-known remedies and penalties for breaches of blockade, where the blockade is real and in fact effective; for trade in contraband;

for every unneutral act by whomsoever attempted. The Government of the United States cannot consent to see these remedies and penalties altered or extended at the will of a single power or group of powers to the injury of its own citizens or in derogation of its own rights. Conspicuous among the principles which the civilized nations of the world have accepted for the safeguarding of the rights of neutrals is the just and honorable principle that neutrals may not be condemned nor their goods confiscated except upon fair adjudication and after an opportunity to be heard, in prize courts or elsewhere. Such safeguards the black list brushes aside. It condemns without hearing, without notice, and in advance. It is manifestly out of the question that the Government of the United States should acquiesce in such methods or applications of punishment to its citizens.

Whatever may be said with regard to the legality, in the view of international obligation, of the act of Parliament upon which the practice of the black list as now employed by His Majesty's Government is understood to be based, the Government of the United States is constrained to regard that practice as inconsistent with that true justice, sincere amity, and impartial fairness which should characterize the dealings of friendly governments with one another. The spirit of reciprocal trade between the United States and Great Britain, the privilege long accorded to the nationals of each to come and go with their ships and cargoes, to use each the other's shipping, and be served each by the other's merchants, is very seriously impaired by arbitrary and sweeping practices such as this. There is no purpose or inclination on the part of the Government of the United States to shield American citizens or business houses in any way from the legitimate consequences of unneutral acts or practices; it is quite willing that they should suffer the appropriate penalties which international law and the usage of nations have sanctioned; but His Britannic Majesty's Government cannot expect the Government of the United States to consent to see its citizens put upon an *ex parte* black list without calling the attention of His Majesty's Government, in the gravest terms, to the many serious consequences to neutral right and neutral relations which such an act must necessarily involve. It hopes and believes that His Majesty's Government, in its natural absorption in a single pressing object of policy, has acted without a full realization of the many undesired and undesirable results that might ensue.

On account of intense feeling aroused here by the publication of British black list it will be necessary to give this note to the press for publication on Saturday morning. Please so explain to British Foreign Office.

POLK

Papers Relating to the Foreign Relations of the
United States, 1916, Supplement (Washington,
1929), pp. 421-2

4   The 'Strict Accountability' Note, February 10, 1915

Defending neutral rights against German submarines proved a most difficult task. The United States set forth its position on the use of this new weapon on February 10, 1915. The note, sent over Secretary of State William J. Bryan's signature, was drafted by Wilson and Robert Lansing, then Counsellor of the State Department.

The Secretary of State to the Ambassador in Germany (Gerard)

[Telegram]

Washington, February 10, 1915, 1 p.m.

1163. Please address a note immediately to the Imperial German Government to the following effect:

The Government of the United States, having had its attention directed to the proclamation of the German Admiralty issued on the 4th of February, that the waters surrounding Great Britain and Ireland, including the whole of the English Channel, are to be considered as comprised within the seat of war; that all enemy merchant vessels found in those waters after the eighteenth instant will be destroyed, although it may not always be possible to save crews and passengers; and that neutral vessels expose themselves to danger within this zone of war because, in view of the misuse of neutral flags said to have been ordered by the British Government on the thirty-first of January and of the contingencies of maritime warfare, it may not be possible always to exempt neutral vessels from attacks intended to strike enemy ships, feels it to be its duty to call the attention of the Imperial German Government, with sincere respect and the most friendly sentiments but very candidly and earnestly, to the very serious possibilities of the course of action apparently contemplated under that proclamation.

The Government of the United States views those possibilities with such grave concern that it feels it to be its privilege, and indeed its duty in the circumstances, to request the Imperial German Government to consider before action is taken the critical situation in respect of the relations between this country and Germany which might arise were the German naval forces, in carrying out the policy foreshadowed in the Admiralty's proclamation, to destroy any merchant vessel of the United States or cause the death of American citizens.

It is of course not necessary to remind the German Government that the sole right of a belligerent in dealing with neutral vessels on the high seas is limited to visit and search, unless a blockade is proclaimed and effectively maintained, which this Government does not understand to be proposed in this case. To declare or exercise a right to attack and destroy any vessel entering a prescribed area of the high seas without first certainly determining its belligerent nationality and the contraband character of its cargo would be an act so unprecedented in naval warfare that this Government is reluctant to believe that the Imperial Government of Germany in this case contemplates it as possible. The suspicion that enemy ships are using neutral flags improperly can create no just presumption that all ships traversing a prescribed area are subject to the same suspicion. It is to determine exactly such questions that this Government understands the right of visit and search to have been recognized.

This Government has carefully noted the explanatory statement issued by the Imperial German Government at the same time with the proclamation of the German Admiralty, and takes this occasion to remind the Imperial German Government very respectfully that the Government of the United States is open to none of the criticisms for unneutral action to which the German Government believe the governments of certain other neutral nations have laid themselves open; that the Government of the United States has not consented to or acquiesced in any measures which may have been taken by the other belligerent nations in the present war which operate to restrain neutral trade, but has, on the contrary, taken in all such matters a position which warrants it in holding those governments responsible in the proper way for any untoward effects upon American shipping which the accepted principles of international law do not justify; and that it, therefore, regards itself as free in the present instance to take with a clear conscience and upon accepted principles the position indicated in this note.

If the commanders of German vessels of war should act upon the presumption that the flag of the United States was not being used in good faith and should destroy on the high seas an American vessel or the lives of American citizens, it would be difficult for the Government of the United States to view the act in any other light than as an indefensible violation of neutral rights which it would be very hard indeed to reconcile with the friendly relations now so happily subsisting between the two Governments.

If such a deplorable situation should arise, the Imperial German Government can readily appreciate that the Government of the United States would be constrained to hold the Imperial German Government to a strict accountability for such acts of their naval authorities and to take any steps it might be necessary to take to safeguard American lives and property and to secure to American citizens the full enjoyment of their acknowledged rights on the high seas.

The Government of the United States, in view of these considerations, which it urges with the greatest respect and with the sincere purpose of making sure that no misunderstanding may arise and no circumstance occur that might even cloud the intercourse of the two Governments, expresses the confident hope and expectation that the Imperial German Government can and will give assurance that American citizens and their vessels will not be molested by the naval forces of Germany otherwise than by visit and search, though their vessels may be traversing the sea area delimited in the proclamation of the German Admiralty.

It is added for the information of the Imperial Government that representations have been made to His Britannic Majesty's Government in respect to the unwarranted use of the American flag for the protection of British ships.

BRYAN

Papers Relating to the Foreign Relations of the United States, 1915, Supplement (Washington, 1928), pp. 98–100

5 The Third 'Lusitania' Note, July 21, 1915

The sinking on May 7, 1915, of the British passenger liner *Lusitania*, and the resultant loss of 1,198 lives (128 American), provoked the first major strain in German–American relations. With public opinion in the United States in white heat against Germany, Wilson struggled to avoid an open break between the two nations, while at the same time demanding cessation of illegal maritime practices. Although two American notes elicited only evasive replies from Berlin, instructions had been issued to U-boat commanders to avoid attacks on passenger vessels. The sinking of another British liner, *Arabic*, on August 19, 1915, severely intensified German–American tension, which was eased when the

German government promised not to attack without warning unarmed passenger vessels.

The Secretary of State to the Ambassador in Germany (Gerard)

[Telegram]

Washington, July 21, 1915, 9 p.m.

1981. You are instructed to deliver textually the following note to the Minister for Foreign Affairs:

The note of the Imperial German Government, dated July 8, 1915, has received the careful consideration of the Government of the United States, and it regrets to be obliged to say that it has found it very unsatisfactory, because it fails to meet the real differences between the two Governments and indicates no way in which the accepted principles of law and humanity may be applied in the grave matter in controversy, but proposes, on the contrary, arrangements for a partial suspension of those principles which virtually set them aside.

The Government of the United States notes with satisfaction that the Imperial German Government recognizes without reservation the validity of the principles insisted on in the several communications which this Government has addressed to the Imperial German Government with regard to its announcement of a war zone and the use of submarines against merchantmen on the high seas—the principle that the high seas are free, that the character and cargo of a merchantman must first be ascertained before she can lawfully be seized or destroyed, and that the lives of non-combatants may in no case be put in jeopardy unless the vessel resists or seeks to escape after being summoned to submit to examination; for a belligerent act of retaliation is *per se* an act beyond the law, and the defense of an act as retaliatory is an admission that it is illegal.

The Government of the United States is, however, keenly disappointed to find that the Imperial German Government regards itself as in large degree exempt from the obligation to observe these principles, even where neutral vessels are concerned, by what it believes the policy and practice of the Government of Great Britain to be in the present war with regard to neutral commerce. The Imperial German Government will readily understand that the Government of the United States can not discuss the policy of the Government of Great Britain with regard to neutral trade except with that Government itself, and that it must regard the conduct of other belligerent governments as irrelevant to any discussion with the Imperial German

Government of what this Government regards as grave and unjustifiable violations of the rights of American citizens by German naval commanders. Illegal and inhuman acts, however justifiable they may be thought to be against an enemy who is believed to have acted in contravention of law and humanity, are manifestly indefensible when they deprive neutrals of their acknowledged rights, particularly when they violate the right to life itself. If a belligerent can not retaliate against an enemy without injuring the lives of neutrals, as well as their property, humanity, as well as justice and a due regard for the dignity of neutral powers, should dictate that the practice be discontinued. If persisted in, it would in such circumstances constitute an unpardonable offense against the sovereignty of the neutral nation affected. The Government of the United States is not unmindful of the extraordinary conditions created by this war or of the radical alterations of circumstance and method of attack produced by the use of instrumentalities of naval warfare which the nations of the world can not have had in view when the existing rules of international law were formulated, and it is ready to make every reasonable allowance for these novel and unexpected aspects of war at sea; but it can not consent to abate any essential or fundamental right of its people because of a mere alteration of circumstance. The rights of neutrals in time of war are based upon principle, not upon expediency, and the principles are immutable. It is the duty and obligation of belligerents to find a way to adapt the new circumstances to them.

The events of the past two months have clearly indicated that it is possible and practicable to conduct such submarine operations as have characterized the activity of the Imperial German Navy within the so-called war zone, in substantial accord with the accepted practices of regulated warfare. The whole world has looked with interest and increasing satisfaction at the demonstration of that possibility by German naval commanders. It is manifestly possible, therefore, to lift the whole practice of submarine attack above the criticism which it has aroused and remove the chief causes of offense.

In view of the admission of illegality made by the Imperial Government when it pleaded the right of retaliation in defense of its acts, and in view of the manifest possibility of conforming to the established rules of naval warfare, the Government of the United States can not believe that the Imperial Government will longer refrain from disavowing the wanton act of its naval commander in sinking the *Lusitania* or from offering reparation for the American lives lost, so far as reparation can be made for a needless destruction of human life by an illegal act.

The Government of the United States, while not indifferent to the friendly spirit in which it is made, can not accept the suggestion of the Imperial German Government that certain vessels be designated and agreed upon which shall be free on the seas now illegally proscribed. The very agreement would, by implication, subject other vessels to illegal attack and would be a curtailment and therefore an abandonment of the principles for which this Government contends and which in times of calmer counsels every nation would concede as of course.

The Government of the United States and the Imperial German Government are contending for the same great object, have long stood together in urging the very principles upon which the Government of the United States now so solemnly insists. They are both contending for the freedom of the seas. The Government of the United States will continue to contend for that freedom, from whatever quarter violated, without compromise and at any cost. It invites the practical cooperation of the Imperial German Government at this time when cooperation may accomplish most and this great common object be most strikingly and effectively achieved.

The Imperial German Government expresses the hope that this object may be in some measure accomplished even before the present war ends. It can be. The Government of the United States not only feels obliged to insist upon it, by whomsoever violated or ignored, in the protection of its own citizens, but is also deeply interested in seeing it made practicable between the belligerents themselves, and holds itself ready at any time to act as the common friend who may be privileged to suggest a way.

In the meantime the very value which this Government sets upon the long and unbroken friendship between the people and Government of the United States and the people and Government of the German nation impels it to press very solemnly upon the Imperial German Government the necessity for a scrupulous observance of neutral rights in this critical matter. Friendship itself prompts it to say to the Imperial Government that repetition by the commanders of German naval vessels of acts in contravention of those rights must be regarded by the Government of the United States, when they affect American citizens, as deliberately unfriendly.

LANSING

Papers Relating to the Foreign Relations of the United States, 1915, Supplement (Washington, 1928), pp. 480-2

6 The 'Sussex' Ultimatum, April 18, 1916

A U-boat attack on the Channel steamer *Sussex* on March 24, 1916, brought Germany and the United States to the verge of war. In an ultimatum to the German government, President Wilson demanded that attacks against unarmed vessels cease immediately. Berlin, after some hesitation, pledged adherence to the rules of international law regarding search and visit, but reserved the right to return to indiscriminate attacks if the United States failed to compel the Allies to observe international law in their own maritime warfare.

The Secretary of State to the Ambassador in Germany (Gerard)

[Telegram]

Washington, April 18, 1916, 6 p.m.

2913. You are instructed to deliver to the Secretary of Foreign Affairs a communication reading as follows:

I did not fail to transmit immediately, by telegraph, to my Government your excellency's note of the 10th instant in regard to certain attacks by German submarines, and particularly in regard to the disastrous explosion which, on March 24 last, wrecked the French S.S. *Sussex* in the English Channel. I have now the honor to deliver, under instructions from my Government, the following reply to your excellency:

Information now in the possession of the Government of the United States fully establishes the facts in the case of the *Sussex*, and the inferences which my Government has drawn from that information it regards as confirmed by the circumstances set forth in your excellency's note of the 10th instant. On the 24th of March 1916, at about 2.50 o'clock in the afternoon, the unarmed steamer *Sussex*, with 325 or more passengers on board, among whom were a number of American citizens, was torpedoed while crossing from Folkestone to Dieppe. The *Sussex* had never been armed; was a vessel known to be habitually used only for the conveyance of passengers across the English Channel; and was not following the route taken by troopships or supply ships. About 80 of her passengers, non-combatants of all ages and sexes, including citizens of the United States, were killed or injured.

A careful, detailed, and scrupulously impartial investigation by naval and military officers of the United States has conclusively established the fact that the *Sussex* was torpedoed without warning or summons to surrender and that the torpedo by which she was struck was of German manufacture. In the view of the Government of the United States these facts from the first made the conclusion that the torpedo was fired by a German submarine unavoidable. It now considers that conclusion substantiated by the statements of your excellency's note. A full statement of the facts upon which the Government of the United States has based its conclusion is enclosed.

The Government of the United States, after having given careful consideration to the note of the Imperial Government of the 10th of April, regrets to state that the impression made upon it by the statements and proposals contained in that note is that the Imperial Government has failed to appreciate the gravity of the situation which has resulted, not alone from the attack on the *Sussex*, but from the whole method and character of submarine warfare as disclosed by the unrestrained practice of the commanders of German undersea craft during the past twelvemonth and more in the indiscriminate destruction of merchant vessels of all sorts, nationalities, and destinations. If the sinking of the *Sussex* had been an isolated case, the Government of the United States might find it possible to hope that the officer who was responsible for that act had wilfully violated his orders or had been criminally negligent in taking none of the precautions they prescribed, and that the ends of justice might be satisfied by imposing upon him an adequate punishment, coupled with a formal disavowal of the act and payment of a suitable indemnity by the Imperial Government. But, though the attack upon the *Sussex* was manifestly indefensible and caused a loss of life so tragical as to make it stand forth as one of the most terrible examples of the inhumanity of submarine warfare as the commanders of German vessels are conducting it, it unhappily does not stand alone.

On the contrary, the Government of the United States is forced by recent events to conclude that it is only one instance, even though one of the most extreme and most distressing instances, of the deliberate method and spirit of indiscriminate destruction of merchant vessels of all sorts, nationalities, and destinations which have become more and more unmistakable as the activity of German undersea vessels of war has in recent months been quickened and extended.

The Imperial Government will recall that when, in February 1915, it announced its intention of treating the waters surrounding Great Britain and Ireland as embraced within the seat of war and of destroying all merchant ships owned by its enemies that might be found within that zone of danger, and warned all vessels, neutral as well as belligerent, to keep out of the waters thus proscribed or to enter them at their peril, the Government of the United States earnestly protested. It took the position that such a policy could not be pursued without constant gross and palpable violations of the accepted law of nations, particularly if submarine craft were to be employed as its instruments, inasmuch as the rules prescribed by that law, rules founded on the principles of humanity and established for the protection of the lives of non-combatants at sea, could not in the nature of the case be observed by such vessels. It based its protest on the ground that persons of neutral nationality and vessels of neutral ownership would be exposed to extreme and intolerable risks; and that no right to close any part of the high seas could lawfully be asserted by the Imperial Government in the circumstances then existing. The law of nations in these matters, upon which the Government of the United States based that protest, is not of recent origin or founded upon merely arbitrary principles set up by convention. It is based, on the contrary, upon manifest principles of humanity and has long been established with the approval and by the express assent of all civilized nations.

The Imperial Government, notwithstanding, persisted in carrying out the policy announced, expressing the hope that the dangers involved, at any rate to neutral vessels, would be reduced to a minimum by the instructions which it had issued to the commanders of its submarines, and assuring the Government of the United States that it would take every possible precaution both to respect the rights of neutrals and to safeguard the lives of non-combatants.

In pursuance of this policy of submarine warfare against the commerce of its adversaries, thus announced and thus entered upon in despite of the solemn protest of the Government of the United States, the commanders of the Imperial Government's undersea vessels have carried on practices of such ruthless destruction which have made it more and more evident as the months have gone by that the Imperial Government has found it impracticable to put any such restraints upon them as it had hoped and promised to put. Again and again the Imperial Government has given its solemn assurances to the Government of the United States that at least passenger ships would not be thus dealt with, and yet it has repeatedly permitted its undersea commanders to disregard those assurances with entire impunity. As recently as February last it gave notice that it would regard all armed merchantmen owned by its enemies as part of the armed naval forces of its adversaries and deal with them as with men-of-war, thus, at least by implication, pledging itself to give warning to vessels which were not armed and to accord security of life to their passengers and crews; but even this limitation its submarine commanders have recklessly ignored.

Vessels of neutral ownership, even vessels of neutral ownership bound from neutral port to neutral port, have been destroyed along with vessels of belligerent ownership in constantly increasing numbers. Sometimes the merchantmen attacked have been warned and summoned to surrender before being fired on or torpedoed; sometimes their passengers and crews have been vouchsafed the poor security of being allowed to take to the ship's boats before the ship was sent to the bottom. But again and again no warning has been given, no escape even to the ship's boats allowed to those on board. Great liners like the *Lusitania* and *Arabic* and mere passenger boats like the *Sussex* have been attacked without a moment's warning, often before they have even become aware that they were in the presence of an armed ship of the enemy, and the lives of non-combatants, passengers, and crew have been destroyed wholesale and in a manner which the Government of the United States can not but regard as wanton and without the slightest color of justification. No limit of any kind has in fact been set to their indiscriminate pursuit and destruction of merchantmen of all kinds and nationalities within the waters which the Imperial Government has chosen to designate as lying within the seat of war. The roll of Americans who have lost their lives upon ships thus attacked and destroyed has grown month by month until the ominous toll has mounted into the hundreds.

The Government of the United States has been very patient. At every stage of this distressing experience of tragedy after tragedy it has sought to be governed by the most thoughtful consideration of the extraordinary circumstances of an unprecedented war and to be guided by sentiments of very genuine friendship for the people and Government of Germany. It has accepted the successive explanations and assurances of the Imperial Government as, of course, given in entire sincerity and good faith, and has hoped, even against hope, that it would prove to be possible for the Imperial Government so to order and control the acts of its naval commanders as to square its policy with the recognized principles of humanity as embodied in the law of nations. It has made every allowance for unprecedented conditions and has been willing to wait until the facts became unmistakable and were susceptible of only one interpretation.

It now owes it to a just regard for its own rights to say to the Imperial Government that that time has come. It has become painfully evident to it that the position which it took at the very outset is inevitable, namely, the use of submarines for the destruction of an enemy's commerce is, of necessity, because of the very character of the vessels employed and the very methods of attack which their employment of course involves, utterly incompatible with the principles of humanity, the long-established and incontrovertible rights of neutrals, and the sacred immunities of non-combatants.

If it is still the purpose of the Imperial Government to prosecute relentless and indiscriminate warfare against vessels of commerce by the use of submarines without regard to what the Government of the United States must consider the sacred and indisputable rules of international law and the universally recognized dictates of humanity, the Government of the United States is at last forced to the conclusion that there is but one course it can pursue. Unless the Imperial Government should now immediately declare and effect an abandonment of its present methods of submarine warfare against passenger and freight-carrying vessels, the Government of the United States can have no choice but to sever diplomatic relations with the German Empire altogether. This action the Government of the United States contemplates with the greatest reluctance but feels constrained to take in behalf of humanity and the rights of neutral nations.

LANSING

Papers Relating to the Foreign Relations of the United States, 1916, Supplement (Washington, 1929), pp. 232-4

VI

THE UNITED STATES AND THE GREAT WAR: THE FAILURE OF MEDIATION

1 The House-Grey Memorandum, February 22, 1916

Wilson, in his efforts to mediate a peace settlement, dispatched Colonel House to Europe in January 1916. Despite House's commitment to Sir Edward Grey, the belligerents refused to consider a negotiated settlement.

'(*Confidential*)
    'Colonel House told me that President Wilson was ready, on hearing from France and England that the moment was opportune, to propose that a Conference should be summoned to put an end to the war. Should the Allies accept this proposal, and should Germany refuse it, the United States would probably enter the war against Germany.
    'Colonel House expressed the opinion that, if such a Conference met, it would secure peace on terms not unfavourable to the Allies; and, if it failed to secure peace, the United States would leave the Conference as a belligerent on the side of the Allies, if Germany was unreasonable. Colonel House expressed an opinion decidedly favourable to the restoration of Belgium, the transfer of Alsace and Lorraine to France, and the acquisition by Russia of an outlet to the sea, though he thought that the loss of territory incurred by Germany in one place would have to be compensated to her by concessions to her in other places outside Europe. If the Allies delayed accepting the offer of President Wilson, and if, later on, the course of the war was so unfavourable to them that the intervention of the United States would not be effective, the United States would probably disinterest themselves in Europe and look to their own protection in their own way.
    'I said that I felt the statement, coming from the President of the

United States, to be a matter of such importance that I must inform the Prime Minister and my colleagues; but that I could say nothing until it had received their consideration. The British Government could, under no circumstances, accept or make any proposal except in consultation and agreement with the Allies. I thought that the Cabinet would probably feel that the present situation would not justify them in approaching their Allies on this subject at the present moment; but, as Colonel House had had an intimate conversation with M. Briand and M. Jules Cambon in Paris, I should think it right to tell M. Briand privately, through the French Ambassador in London, what Colonel House had said to us; and I should, of course, whenever there was an opportunity, be ready to talk the matter over with M. Briand, if he desired it.'

House Papers, Yale University Library

2 President Wilson defines the 'Essential Terms of Peace in Europe', January 22, 1917

Disturbed by the attitude of the belligerents, who refused to offer any specific proposals for a negotiated peace, Wilson offered his own statement of principles upon which a European peace could be based. But this effort also proved futile. Germany, in fact, had already decided to launch a campaign of unrestricted submarine warfare.

GENTLEMEN OF THE SENATE:

On the eighteenth of December last I addressed an identic note to the governments of the nations now at war requesting them to state, more definitely than they had yet been stated by either group of belligerents, the terms upon which they would deem it possible to make peace. I spoke on behalf of humanity and of the rights of all neutral nations like our own, many of whose most vital interests the war puts in constant jeopardy. The Central Powers united in a reply which stated merely that they were ready to meet their antagonists in conference to discuss terms of peace. The Entente Powers have replied much more definitely and have stated, in general terms, indeed, but with sufficient definiteness to imply details, the arrangements, guarantees, and acts of reparation which they deem to be the indispensable conditions of a satisfactory settlement. We are that much nearer a definite discussion of the peace which shall end the present war. We are that much nearer the discussion of the international concert which must thereafter hold the world at peace. In every discussion of the peace that must end this war it is taken for granted that that peace must be followed by some definite concert of power which will make it virtually impossible that any such catastrophe should ever overwhelm us again. Every lover of mankind, every sane and thoughtful man must take that for granted.

I have sought this opportunity to address you because I thought that I owed it to you, as the counsel associated with me in the final determination of our international obligations, to disclose to you without reserve the thought and purpose that have been taking form in my mind in regard to the duty of our Government in the days to come when it will be necessary to lay afresh and upon a new plan the foundations of peace among the nations.

It is inconceivable that the people of the United States should play no part in that great enterprise. To take part in such a service will be the opportunity for which they have sought to prepare themselves by the very principles and purposes of their polity and the approved practices of their Government ever since the days when they set up a new nation in the high and honorable hope that it might in all that it was and did show mankind the way to liberty. They cannot in honor withhold the service to which they are now about to be challenged. They do not wish to withhold it. But they owe it to themselves and to the other nations of the world to state the conditions under which they will feel free to render it.

That service is nothing less than this, to add their authority and their power to the authority and force of other nations to guarantee peace and justice throughout the world.   Such a settlement cannot now be long postponed. It is right that before it comes this Government should frankly formulate the conditions upon which it would feel justified in asking our people to approve its formal and solemn adherence to a League for Peace. I am here to attempt to state those conditions.

The present war must first be ended; but we owe it to candor and to a just regard for the opinion of mankind to say that, so far as our participation in guarantees of future peace is concerned, it makes a great deal of difference in what way and upon what terms it is ended. The treaties and agreements which bring it to an end must embody terms which will create a peace that is worth guaranteeing and preserving, a peace that will win the approval of mankind, not merely a peace that will serve the several interests and immediate aims of the nations engaged. We shall have no voice in determining what those terms shall be, but we shall, I feel sure, have a voice in determining whether they shall be made lasting or not by the guarantees of a universal covenant, and our judgment upon what is fundamental and essential as a condition precedent to permanency should be spoken now, not afterwards when it may be too late.

No covenant of co-operative peace that does not include the peoples of the New World can suffice to keep the future safe against war; and yet there is only one sort of peace that the peoples of America could join in guaranteeing. The elements of that peace must be elements that engage the confidence and satisfy the principles of the American governments, elements consistent with their political faith and with the practical convictions which the peoples of America have once for all embraced and undertaken to defend.

I do not mean to say that any American government would throw any obstacle in the way of any terms of peace the governments now at war might agree upon, or seek to upset them when made, whatever they might be. I only take it for granted that mere terms of peace between the belligerents will not satisfy even the belligerents themselves. Mere agreements may not make peace secure. It will be absolutely necessary that a force be created as a guarantor of the permanency of the settlement so much greater than the force of any nation now engaged or any alliance hitherto formed or projected that no nation, no probable combination of nations could face or withstand it. If the peace presently to be made is to endure, it must be a peace made secure by the organized major force of mankind.

The terms of the immediate peace agreed upon will determine whether it is a peace for which such a guarantee can be secured. The question upon which the whole future peace and policy of the world depends is this: Is the present war a struggle for a just and secure peace, or only for a new balance of power? If it be only a struggle for a new balance of power, who will guarantee, who can guarantee the stable equilibrium of the new arrangement? Only a tranquil Europe can be a stable Europe. There must be, not a balance of power, but a community of power; not organized rivalries, but an organized common peace.

Fortunately we have received very explicit assurances on this point. The statesmen of both of the groups of nations now arrayed against one another have said, in terms that could not be misinterpreted, that it was no part of the purpose they had in mind to crush their antagonists. But the implications of these assurances may not be equally clear to all – may not be the same on both sides of the water. I think it will be serviceable if I attempt to set forth what we understand them to be.

They imply, first of all, that it must be a peace without victory. It is not pleasant to say this. I beg that I may be permitted to put my own interpretation upon it and that it may be understood that no other interpretation was in my thought. I am seeking only to face realities and to face them without soft concealments. Victory would mean peace forced upon the loser, a victor's terms imposed upon the vanquished. It would be accepted in humiliation, under duress, at an intolerable sacrifice, and would leave a sting, a resentment, a bitter memory upon which terms of peace would rest, not permanently, but only as upon quicksand. Only a peace between equals can last. Only a peace the very principle of which is equality and a common participation in a common benefit. The right state of mind, the right feeling between nations, is as necessary for a lasting peace as is the just settlement of vexed questions of territory or of racial and national allegiance.

The equality of nations upon which peace must be founded if it is to last must be an equality of rights; the guarantees exchanged must neither recognize nor imply a difference between big nations and small, between those that are powerful and those that are weak. Right must be based upon the common strength, not upon the individual strength, of the nations upon whose concert peace will depend. Equality of territory or of resources there of course cannot be; nor any other sort of equality not gained in the ordinary peaceful and legitimate development of the peoples themselves. But no one asks or expects anything more than an equality of rights. Mankind is looking now for freedom of life, not for equipoises of power.

And there is a deeper thing involved than even equality of right among organized nations. No peace can last, or ought to last, which does not recognize and accept the principle that governments derive all their just powers from the consent of the governed, and that no right anywhere exists to hand peoples about from sovereignty to sovereignty as if they were property. I take it for granted, for instance, if I may venture upon a single example, that statesmen everywhere are agreed that there should be a united, independent, and autonomous Poland, and that henceforth inviolable security of life, of worship, and of industrial and social development should be guaranteed to all peoples who have lived hitherto under the power of governments devoted to a faith and purpose hostile to their own.

I speak of this, not because of any desire to exalt an abstract political principle which has always been held very dear by those who have sought to build up liberty in America, but for the same reason that I have spoken of the other conditions of peace which seem to me clearly indispensable – because I wish frankly to uncover realities. Any peace which does not recognize and accept this principle will inevitably be upset. It will not rest upon the affections or the convictions of mankind. The ferment of spirit of whole populations will fight subtly and constantly against it, and all the world will sympathize. The world can be at peace only if its life is stable, and there can be no stability where the will is in rebellion, where there is not tranquility of spirit and a sense of justice, of freedom, and of right.

So far as practicable, moreover, every great people now struggling towards a full development of its resources and of its powers should be assured a direct outlet to the great highways of the sea. Where this cannot be done by the cession of territory, it can no doubt be done by the neutralization of direct rights of way under the general guarantee which will assure the peace itself. With a right comity of arrangement no nation need be shut away from free access to the open paths of the world's commerce.

And the paths of the sea must alike in law and in fact be free. The freedom of the seas is the *sine qua non* of peace, equality, and co-operation. No doubt a somewhat radical reconsideration of many of the rules of international practice hitherto thought to be established may be necessary in order to make the seas indeed free and common in practically all circumstances for the use of mankind, but the motive for such changes is convincing and compelling. There can be no trust or intimacy between the peoples of the world without them. The free, constant, unthreatened intercourse of nations is an essential part of the process of peace and of development. It need not be difficult either to define or to secure the freedom of the seas if the governments of the world sincerely desire to come to an agreement concerning it.

It is a problem closely connected with the limitation of naval armaments and the co-operation of the navies of the world in keeping the seas at once free and safe. And the question of limiting naval armaments opens the wider and perhaps more difficult question of the limitation of armies and of all programs of military preparation. Difficult and delicate as these questions are, they must be faced with the utmost candor and decided in a spirit of real accommodation if peace is to come with healing in its wings, and come to stay. Peace cannot be had without concession and sacrifice. There can be no sense of safety and equality among the nations if great preponderating armaments are henceforth to continue here and there to be built up and maintained. The statesmen of the world must plan for peace and nations must adjust and accommodate their policy to it as they have planned for war

and made ready for pitiless contest and rivalry. The question of armaments, whether on land or sea, is the most immediately and intensely
practical question connected with the future fortunes of nations and of
mankind.

I have spoken upon these great matters without reserve and with the
utmost explicitness because it has seemed to me to be necessary if the
world's yearning desire for peace was anywhere to find free voice and
utterance. Perhaps I am the only person in high authority amongst all
the peoples of the world who is at liberty to speak and hold nothing
back. I am speaking as an individual, and yet I am speaking also, of
course, as the responsible head of a great government, and I feel confident that I have said what the people of the United States would wish
me to say. May I not add that I hope and believe that I am in effect
speaking for liberals and friends of humanity in every nation and of
every program of liberty? I would fain believe that I am speaking for
the silent mass of mankind everywhere who have as yet had no place
or opportunity to speak their real hearts out concerning the death and
ruin they see to have come already upon the persons and the homes
they hold most dear.

And in holding out the expectation that the people and Government
of the United States will join the other civilized nations of the world in
guaranteeing the permanence of peace upon such terms as I have named
I speak with the greater boldness and confidence because it is clear to
every man who can think that there is in this promise no breach in
either our traditions or our policy as a nation, but a fulfilment, rather,
of all that we have professed or striven for.

I am proposing, as it were, that the nations should with one accord
adopt the doctrine of President Monroe as the doctrine of the world:
that no nation should seek to extend its polity over any other nation or
people, but that every people should be left free to determine its own
polity, its own way of development, unhindered, unthreatened, un-
afraid, the little along with the great and powerful.

I am proposing that all nations henceforth avoid entangling alliances
which would draw them into competitions of power; catch them in a
net of intrigue and selfish rivalry, and disturb their own affairs with
influences intruded from without. There is no entangling alliance in a
concert of power. When all unite to act in the same sense and with the
same purpose all act in the common interest and are free to live their
own lives under a common protection.

I am proposing government by the consent of the governed; that
freedom of the seas which in international conference after conference

representatives of the United States have urged with the eloquence of those who are the convinced disciples of liberty; and that moderation of armaments which makes of armies and navies a power for order merely, not an instrument of aggression or of selfish violence.

These are American principles, American policies. We could stand for no others. And they are also the principles and policies of forward looking men and women everywhere, of every modern nation, of every enlightened community. They are the principles of mankind and must prevail.

> 'Essential Terms of Peace in Europe: Address to the United States Senate, January 22, 1917.' *The Public Papers of Woodrow Wilson: The New Democracy*, ed. Ray Stannard Baker and William E. Dodd (2 vols., New York, 1926), II, pp. 407-14

3   President Wilson's War Message, April 2, 1917

Wilson learned of Germany's decision for an all-out U-boat offensive on January 31. Diplomatic relations were severed three days later. The destruction of American ships brought Wilson before Congress on April 2. Germany's violation of neutral rights caused America's entry into the war. But, as Wilson explained to Congress, even more fundamental issues were at stake.

I have called the Congress into extraordinary session because there are serious, very serious, choices of policy to be made, and made immediately, which it was neither right nor constitutionally permissible that I should assume the responsibility of making.

On the third of February last I officially laid before you the extraordinary announcement of the Imperial German Government that on and after the first day of February it was its purpose to put aside all restraints of law or of humanity and use its submarines to sink every vessel that sought to approach either the ports of Great Britain and Ireland or the western coasts of Europe or any of the ports controlled by the enemies of Germany within the Mediterranean. That had seemed to be the object of the German submarine warfare earlier in the war, but since April of last year the Imperial Government had somewhat restrained the commanders of its undersea craft in conformity with its promise then given to us that passenger boats should not be sunk and that due warning would be given to all other vessels which its submarines might seek to destroy, when no resistance was offered or escape attempted, and care taken that their crews were given at least a fair chance to save their lives in their open boats. The precautions taken were meager and haphazard enough, as was proved in distressing instance after instance in the progress of the cruel and unmanly business, but a certain degree of restraint was observed. The new policy has swept every restriction aside. Vessels of every kind, whatever their flag, their character, their cargo, their destination, their errand, have been ruthlessly sent to the bottom without warning and without thought of help or mercy for those on board, the vessels of friendly neutrals along with those of belligerents. Even hospital ships and ships carrying relief to the sorely bereaved and stricken people of Belgium, though the latter were provided with safe conduct through the proscribed areas by the German Government itself and were distinguished by unmistakable marks of identity, have been sunk with the same reckless lack of compassion or of principle.

I was for a little while unable to believe that such things would in fact be done by any government that had hitherto subscribed to the humane practices of civilized nations. International law had its origin in the attempt to set up some law which would be respected and observed upon the seas, where no nation had right of dominion and where lay the free highways of the world. By painful stage after stage has that law been built up, with meager enough results, indeed, after all was accomplished that could be accomplished, but always with a clear view, at least, of what the heart and conscience of mankind demanded. This minimum of right the German Government has swept aside under the plea of retaliation and necessity and because it had no weapons which it could use at sea except these which it is impossible to employ as it is employing them without throwing to the winds all scruples of humanity or of respect for the understandings that were supposed to underlie the intercourse of the world. I am not now thinking of the loss of property involved, immense and serious as that is, but only of the wanton and wholesale destruction of the lives of non-combatants, men, women, and children, engaged in pursuits which have always, even in the darkest periods of modern history, been deemed innocent and legitimate. Property can be paid for: the lives of peaceful and innocent people cannot be. The present German submarine warfare against commerce is a warfare against mankind.

It is a war against all nations. American ships have been sunk, American lives taken, in ways which it has stirred us very deeply to learn of, but the ships and people of other neutral and friendly nations have been sunk and overwhelmed in the waters in the same way. There has been no discrimination. The challenge is to all mankind. Each nation must decide for itself how it will meet it. The choice we make for ourselves must be made with a moderation of counsel and a temperateness of judgment befitting our character and our motives as a nation. We must put excited feeling away. Our motive will not be revenge or the victorious assertion of the physical might of the nation, but only the vindication of right, of human right, of which we are only a single champion.

When I addressed the Congress on the twenty-sixth of February last I thought that it would suffice to assert our neutral rights with arms, our right to use the seas against unlawful interference, our right to keep our people safe against unlawful violence. But armed neutrality, it now appears, is impracticable. Because submarines are in effect outlaws when used as the German submarines have been used against merchant shipping, it is impossible to defend ships against their attacks as the law of nations has assumed that merchantmen would defend themselves against privateers or cruisers, visible craft giving chase upon the open sea. It is common prudence in such circumstances, grim necessity indeed, to endeavor to destroy them before they have shown their own intention. They must be dealt with upon sight, if dealt with at all. The German Government denies the right of neutrals to use arms at all within the areas of the sea which it has proscribed, even in the defense of rights which no modern publicist has ever before questioned their right to defend. The intimation is conveyed that the armed guards which we have placed on our merchant ships will be treated as beyond the pale of law and subject to be dealt with as pirates would be. Armed neutrality is ineffectual enough at best; in such circumstances and in the face of such pretensions it is worse than ineffectual: it is likely only to produce what it was meant to prevent; it is practically certain to draw us into the war without either the rights or the effectiveness of belligerents. There is one choice we cannot make, we are incapable of making: we will not choose the path of submission and suffer the most sacred rights of our Nation and our people to be ignored or violated. The wrongs against which we now array ourselves are no common wrongs; they cut to the very roots of human life.

With a profound sense of the solemn and even tragical character of the step I am taking and of the grave responsibilities which it involves, but in unhesitating obedience to what I deem my constitutional duty, I advise that the Congress declare the recent course of the Imperial German Government to be in fact nothing less than war against the government and people of the United States; that it formally accept the status of belligerent which has thus been thrust upon it; and that it take immediate steps not only to put the country in a more thorough state of defense but also to exert all its power and employ all its resources to bring the Government of the German Empire to terms and end the war.

What this will involve is clear. It will involve the utmost practicable coöperation in counsel and action with the governments now at war with Germany, and, as incident to that, the extension to those governments of the most liberal financial credits, in order that our resources may so far as possible be added to theirs. It will involve the organization and mobilization of all the material resources of the country to supply the materials of war and serve the incidental needs of the Nation in the most abundant and yet the most economical and efficient way possible. It will involve the immediate full equipment of the navy in all respects but particularly in supplying it with the best means of dealing with the enemy's submarines. It will involve the immediate addition to the armed forces of the United States already provided for by law in case of war at least five hundred thousand men, who should, in my opinion, be chosen upon the principle of universal liability to service, and also the authorization of subsequent additional increments of equal force so soon as they may be needed and can be handled in training. It will involve also, of course, the granting of adequate credits to the Government, sustained, I hope, so far as they can equitably be sustained by the present generation, by well conceived taxation.

I say sustained so far as may be equitable by taxation because it seems to me that it would be most unwise to base the credits which will now be necessary entirely on money borrowed. It is our duty, I most respectfully urge, to protect our people so far as we may against the very serious hardships and evils which would be likely to arise out of the inflation which would be produced by vast loans.

In carrying out the measures by which these things are to be accomplished we should keep constantly in mind the wisdom of interfering as little as possible in our own preparation and in the equipment of our own military forces with the duty – for it will be a very practical duty – of supplying the nations already at war with Germany with the materials which they can obtain only from us or by our assistance. They are in the field and we should help them in every way to be effective there.

I shall take the liberty of suggesting, through the several executive departments of the Government, for the consideration of your committees, measures for the accomplishment of the several objects I have mentioned. I hope that it will be your pleasure to deal with them as having been framed after very careful thought by the branch of the Government upon which the responsibility of conducting the war and safeguarding the Nation will most directly fall.

While we do these things, these deeply momentous things, let us be very clear, and make very clear to all the world what our motives and our objects are. My own thought has not been driven from its habitual and normal course by the unhappy events of the last two months, and I do not believe that the thought of the Nation has been altered or clouded by them. I have exactly the same things in mind now that I had in mind when I addressed the Senate on the twenty-second of January last; the same that I had in mind when I addressed the Congress on the third of February and on the twenty-sixth of February. Our object now, as then, is to vindicate the principles of peace and justice in the life of the world as against selfish and autocratic power and to set up amongst the really free and self-governed peoples of the world such a concert of purpose and of action as will henceforth insure the observance of those principles. Neutrality is no longer feasible or desirable where the peace of the world is involved and the freedom of its peoples, and the menace to that peace and freedom lies in the existence of autocratic governments backed by organized force which is controlled wholly by their will, not by the will of their people. We have seen the last of neutrality in such circumstances. We are at the beginning of an age in which it will be insisted that the same standards of conduct and of responsibility for wrong done shall be observed among nations and their governments that are observed among the individual citizens of civilized states.

We have no quarrel with the German people. We have no feeling towards them but one of sympathy and friendship. It was not upon their impulse that their government acted in entering this war. It was not with their previous knowledge or approval. It was a war determined upon as wars used to be determined upon in the old, unhappy days when peoples were nowhere consulted by their rulers and wars were provoked and waged in the interest of dynasties or of little groups of ambitious men who were accustomed to use their fellow men as pawns and tools. Self-governed nations do not fill their neighbor states with spies or set the course of intrigue to bring about some critical posture of affairs which will give them an opportunity to strike and make conquest. Such designs can be successfully worked out only under cover and where no one has the right to ask questions. Cunningly contrived plans of deception or aggression, carried, it may be, from generation to generation, can be worked out and kept from the light only within the privacy of courts or behind the carefully guarded confidences of a narrow and privileged class. They are happily impossible where public opinion commands and insists upon full information concerning all the nation's affairs.

A steadfast concert for peace can never be maintained except by a partnership of democratic nations. No autocratic government could be trusted to keep faith within it or observe its covenants. It must be a league of honor, a partnership of opinion. Intrigue would eat its vitals away; the plottings of inner circles who could plan what they would and render account to no one would be a corruption seated at its very heart. Only free peoples can hold their purpose and their honor steady to a common end and prefer the interests of mankind to any narrow interest of their own.

Does not every American feel that assurance has been added to our hope for the future peace of the world by the wonderful and heartening things that have been happening within the last few weeks in Russia? Russia was known by those who knew it best to have been always in fact democratic at heart, in all the vital habits of her thought, in all the intimate relationships of her people that spoke their natural instinct, their habitual attitude towards life. The autocracy that crowned the summit of her political structure, long as it had stood and terrible as was the reality of its power, was not in fact Russian in origin, character, or purpose; and now it has been shaken off and the great, generous Russian people have been added in all their naïve majesty and might to the forces that are fighting for freedom in the world, for justice, and for peace. Here is a fit partner for a League of Honor.

One of the things that has served to convince us that the Prussian autocracy was not and could never be our friend is that from the very outset of the present war it has filled our unsuspecting communities and even our offices of government with spies and set criminal intrigues everywhere afoot against our national unity of counsel, our peace within and without, our industries and our commerce. Indeed, it is now evident that its spies were here even before the war began; and it is unhappily not a matter of conjecture but a fact proved in our courts of justice that the intrigues which have more than once come perilously near to disturbing the peace and dislocating the industries of the country have been carried on at the instigation, with the support, and even under the personal direction of official agents of the Imperial Government accredited to the Government of the United States. Even in checking these things and trying to extirpate them we have sought to put the most generous interpretation possible upon them because we know that their source lay not in any hostile feeling or purpose of the German people towards us (who were no doubt as ignorant of them as we ourselves were), but only in the selfish designs of a Government that did what it pleased and told its people nothing. But they have played their part in serving to convince us at last that that Government entertains no real friendship for us and means to act against our peace and security at its convenience. That it means to stir up enemies against us at our very doors the intercepted note to the German Minister at Mexico City is eloquent evidence.

We are accepting this challenge of hostile purpose because we know that in such a Government, following such methods, we can never have a friend; and that in the presence of its organized power, always lying in wait to accomplish we know not what purpose, there can be no assured security for the democratic Governments of the world. We are now about to accept gage of battle with this natural foe to liberty and shall, if necessary, spend the whole force of the Nation to check and nullify its pretensions and its power. We are glad, now that we see the facts with no veil of false pretense about them, to fight thus for the ultimate peace of the world and for the liberation of its peoples, the German peoples included: for the rights of nations great and small and the privilege of men everywhere to choose their way of life and of obedience. The world must be made safe for democracy. Its peace must be planted upon the tested foundations of political liberty. We have no selfish ends to serve. We desire no conquest, no dominion. We seek no indemnities for ourselves, no material compensation for the sacrifices we shall freely make. We are but one of the champions of the rights of mankind. We shall be satisfied when those rights have been made as secure as the faith and the freedom of nations can make them.

Just because we fight without rancor and without selfish object, seeking nothing for ourselves but what we shall wish to share with all free peoples, we shall, I feel confident, conduct our operations as belligerents without passion and ourselves observe with proud punctilio the principles of right and of fair play we profess to be fighting for.

I have said nothing of the Governments allied with the Imperial Government of Germany because they have not made war upon us or challenged us to defend our right and our honor. The Austro-Hungarian Government has, indeed, avowed its unqualified indorsement and acceptance of the reckless and lawless submarine warfare adopted now without disguise by the Imperial German Government, and it has therefore not been possible for this Government to receive Count

Tarnowski, the Ambassador recently accredited to this Government by the Imperial and Royal Government of Austria-Hungary; but that Government has not actually engaged in warfare against citizens of the United States on the seas, and I take the liberty, for the present at least, of postponing a discussion of our relations with the authorities at Vienna. We enter this war only where we are clearly forced into it because there are no other means of defending our rights.

It will be all the easier for us to conduct ourselves as belligerents in a high spirit of right and fairness because we act without animus, not in enmity towards a people or with the desire to bring any injury or dis-advantage upon them, but only in armed opposition to an irresponsible government which has thrown aside all considerations of humanity and of right and is running amuck. We are, let me say again, the sincere friends of the German people, and shall desire nothing so much as the early reëstablishment of intimate relations of mutual advantage between us, – however hard it may be for them, for the time being, to believe that this is spoken from our hearts. We have borne with their present Government through all these bitter months because of that friend-ship, – exercising a patience and forbearance which would otherwise have been impossible. We shall, happily, still have an opportunity to prove that friendship in our daily attitude and actions towards the millions of men and women of German birth and native sympathy who live amongst us and share our life, and we shall be proud to prove it towards all who are in fact loyal to their neighbors and to the Government in the hour of test. They are, most of them, as true and loyal Americans as if they had never known any other fealty or allegiance. They will be prompt to stand with us in rebuking and restraining the few who may be of a different mind and purpose. If there should be disloyalty, it will be dealt with with a firm hand of stern repression; but, if it lifts its head at all, it will lift it only here and there and without countenance except from a lawless and malignant few.

It is a distressing and oppressive duty, Gentlemen of the Congress, which I have performed in thus addressing you. There are, it may be, many months of fiery trial and sacrifice ahead of us. It is a fearful thing to lead this great peaceful people into war, into the most terrible and disastrous of all wars, civilization itself seeming to be in the balance. But the right is more precious than peace, and we shall fight for the things which we have always carried nearest our hearts, – for demo-cracy, for the right of those who submit to authority to have a voice in their own Governments, for the rights and liberties of small nations, for a universal dominion of right by such a concert of free peoples as shall bring peace and safety to all nations and make the world itself at last free. To such a task we can dedicate our lives and our fortunes, everything that we are and everything that we have, with the pride of those who know that the day has come when America is privileged to spend her blood and her might for the principles that gave her birth and happiness and the peace which she has treasured. God helping her, she can do no other.

'For Declaration of War Against Germany: Address Delivered at a Joint Session of the Two Houses of Congress, April 2, 1917.' *The Public Papers of Woodrow Wilson: War and Peace*, ed. Ray Stannard Baker and William E. Dodd (2 vols., New York, 1927), I, pp. 6-16

VII

THE UNITED STATES AND
THE GREAT WAR:
WAR AND PEACE

1 President Wilson's 'Fourteen Points',
January 8, 1918

The demand for a statement of Allied and American war aims became urgent
following the publication by the Bolshevik government of the secret treaties
existing among the Allies. When an Inter-Allied Conference, meeting in Paris
in November-December 1917, became deadlocked over the question of war
aims, Wilson decided to issue his own statement on the subject.

Once more, as repeatedly before, the spokesmen of the Central
Empires have indicated their desire to discuss the objects of the war and
the possible bases of a general peace. Parleys have been in progress at
Brest-Litovsk between representatives of the Central Powers to which
the attention of all the belligerents has been invited for the purpose of
ascertaining whether it may be possible to extend these parleys into a
general conference with regard to terms of peace and settlement. The
Russian representatives presented not only a perfectly definite statement of the principles upon which they would be willing to conclude
peace but also an equally definite program of the concrete application
of those principles. The representatives of the Central Powers, on their
part, presented an outline of settlement which, if much less definite,
seemed susceptible of liberal interpretation until their specific program
of practical terms was added. That program proposed no concessions
at all either to the sovereignty of Russia or to the preferences of the
populations with whose fortunes it dealt, but meant, in a word, that
the Central Empires were to keep every foot of territory their armed
forces had occupied, – every province, every city, every point of
vantage, – as a permanent addition to their territories and their power.
It is a reasonable conjecture that the general principles of settlement

which they at first suggested originated with the more liberal statesmen of Germany and Austria, the men who have begun to feel the force of their own peoples' thought and purpose, while the concrete terms of actual settlement came from the military leaders who have no thought but to keep what they have got. The negotiations have been broken off. The Russian representatives were sincere and in earnest. They cannot entertain such proposals of conquest and domination.

The whole incident is full of significance. It is also full of perplexity. With whom are the Russian representatives dealing? For whom are the representatives of the Central Empires speaking? Are they speaking for the majorities of their respective parliaments or for the minority parties, that military and imperialistic minority which has so far dominated their whole policy and controlled the affairs of Turkey and of the Balkan states which have felt obliged to become their associates in this war? The Russian representatives have insisted very justly, very wisely, and in the true spirit of modern democracy, that the conferences they have been holding with the Teutonic and Turkish statesmen should be held within open, not closed, doors, and all the world has been audience, as was desired. To whom have we been listening, then? To those who speak the spirit and intention of the Resolutions of the German Reichstag of the ninth of July last, the spirit and intention of the liberal leaders and parties of Germany, or to those who resist and defy that spirit and intention and insist upon conquest and subjugation? Or are we listening, in fact, to both, unreconciled and in open and hopeless contradiction? These are very serious and pregnant questions. Upon the answer to them depends the peace of the world.

But, whatever the results of the parleys at Brest-Litovsk, whatever the confusions of counsel and of purpose in the utterances of the spokesmen of the Central Empires, they have again attempted to acquaint the world with their objects in the war and have again challenged their adversaries to say what their objects are and what sort of settlement they would deem just and satisfactory. There is no good reason why that challenge should not be responded to, and responded to with the utmost candor. We did not wait for it. Not once, but again and again, we have laid our whole thought and purpose before the world, not in general terms only, but each time with sufficient definition to make it clear what sort of definitive terms of settlement must necessarily spring out of them. Within the last week Mr. Lloyd George has spoken with admirable candor and in admirable spirit for the people and Government of Great Britain. There is no confusion of counsel among the adversaries of the Central Powers, no uncertainty of principle, no vagueness of detail. The only secrecy of counsel, the only lack of fearless frankness, the only failure to make definite statement of the objects of the war, lies with Germany and her Allies. The issues of life and death hang upon these definitions. No statesman who has the least conception of his responsibility ought for a moment to permit himself to continue this tragical and appalling outpouring of blood and treasure unless he is sure beyond a peradventure that the objects of the vital sacrifice are part and parcel of the very life of Society and that the people for whom he speaks think them right and imperative as he does.

There is, moreover, a voice calling for these definitions of principle and of purpose which is, it seems to me, more thrilling and more compelling than any of the many moving voices with which the troubled air of the world is filled. It is the voice of the Russian people. They are prostrate and all but helpless, it would seem, before the grim power of Germany, which has hitherto known no relenting and no pity. Their power, apparently, is shattered. And yet their soul is not subservient. They will not yield either in principle or in action. Their conception of what is right, of what it is humane and honorable for them to accept, has been stated with a frankness, a largeness of view, a generosity of spirit, and a universal human sympathy which must challenge the admiration of every friend of mankind; and they have refused to compound their ideals or desert others that they themselves may be safe. They call to us to say what it is that we desire, in what, if in anything, our purpose and our spirit differ from theirs; and I believe that the people of the United States would wish me to respond, with utter simplicity and frankness. Whether their present leaders believe it or not, it is our heartfelt desire and hope that some way may be opened whereby we may be privileged to assist the people of Russia to attain their utmost hope of liberty and ordered peace.

It will be our wish and purpose that the processes of peace, when they are begun, shall be absolutely open and that they shall involve and permit henceforth no secret understandings of any kind. The day of conquest and aggrandizement is gone by; so is also the day of secret covenants entered into in the interest of particular governments and likely at some unlooked-for moment to upset the peace of the world. It is this happy fact, now clear to the view of every public man whose thoughts do not still linger in an age that is dead and gone, which makes it possible for every nation whose purposes are consistent with justice and the peace of the world to avow now or at any other time the objects it has in view.

We entered this war because violations of right had occurred which touched us to the quick and made the life of our own people impossible unless they were corrected and the world secured once for all against their recurrence. What we demand in this war, therefore, is nothing peculiar to ourselves. It is that the world be made fit and safe to live in; and particularly that it be made safe for every peace-loving nation which, like our own, wishes to live its own life, determine its own institutions, be assured of justice and fair dealing by the other peoples of the world as against force and selfish aggression. All the peoples of the world are in effect partners in this interest, and for our own part we see very clearly that unless justice be done to others it will not be done to us. The program of the world's peace, therefore, is our program; and that program, the only possible program, as we see it, is this:

I Open covenants of peace, openly arrived at, after which there shall be no private international understandings of any kind but diplomacy shall proceed always frankly and in the public view.

II Absolute freedom of navigation upon the seas, outside territorial waters, alike in peace and in war, except as the seas may be closed in whole or in part by international action for the enforcement of international covenants.

III The removal, so far as possible, of all economic barriers and the establishment of an equality of trade conditions among all the nations consenting to the peace and associating themselves for its maintenance.

IV Adequate guarantees given and taken that national armaments will be reduced to the lowest point consistent with domestic safety.

V A free, open-minded, and absolutely impartial adjustment of all colonial claims, based upon a strict observance of the principle that in determining all such questions of sovereignty the interests of the populations concerned must have equal weight with the equitable claims of the government whose title is to be determined.

VI The evacuation of all Russian territory and such a settlement of all questions affecting Russia as will secure the best and freest coöperation of the other nations of the world in obtaining for her an unhampered and unembarrassed opportunity for the independent determination of her own political development and national policy and assure her of a sincere welcome into the society of free nations under institutions of her own choosing; and, more than a welcome, assistance also of every kind that she may need and may herself desire. The treatment accorded Russia by her sister nations in the months to come will be the acid test of their good will, of their comprehension of her needs as distinguished from their own interests, and of their intelligent and unselfish sympathy.

VII Belgium, the whole world will agree, must be evacuated and restored, without any attempt to limit the sovereignty which she enjoys in common with all other free nations. No other single act will serve as this will serve to restore confidence among the nations in the laws which they have themselves set and determined for the government of their relations with one another. Without this healing act the whole structure and validity of international law is forever impaired.

VIII All French territory should be freed and the invaded portions restored, and the wrong done to France by Prussia in 1871 in the matter of Alsace-Lorraine, which has unsettled the peace of the world for nearly fifty years, should be righted, in order that peace may once more be made secure in the interest of all.

IX A readjustment of the frontiers of Italy should be effected along clearly recognizable lines of nationality.

X The peoples of Austria-Hungary, whose place among the nations we wish to see safeguarded and assured, should be accorded the freest opportunity of autonomous development.

XI Rumania, Serbia, and Montenegro should be evacuated; occupied territories restored; Serbia accorded free and secure access to the sea; and the relations of the several Balkan states to one another determined by friendly counsel along historically established lines of allegiance and nationality; and international guarantees of the political and economic independence and territorial integrity of the several Balkan states should be entered into.

XII The Turkish portions of the present Ottoman Empire should be assured a secure sovereignty, but the other nationalities which are now under Turkish rule should be assured an undoubted security of life and an absolutely unmolested opportunity of autonomous development, and the Dardanelles should be permanently opened as a free passage to the ships and commerce of all nations under international guarantees.

XIII An independent Polish state should be erected which should include the territories inhabited by indisputably Polish populations, which should be assured a free and secure access to the sea, and whose political and economic independence and territorial integrity should be guaranteed by international covenant.

XIV A general association of nations must be formed under specific covenants for the purpose of affording mutual guarantees of political independence and territorial integrity to great and small states alike.

In regard to these essential rectifications of wrong and assertions of right we feel ourselves to be intimate partners of all the governments and peoples associated together against the Imperialists. We cannot be separated in interest or divided in purpose. We stand together until the end.

For such arrangements and covenants we are willing to fight and to continue to fight until they are achieved; but only because we wish the right to prevail and desire a just and stable peace such as can be secured only by removing the chief provocations to war, which this program does remove. We have no jealousy of German greatness, and there is nothing in this program that impairs it. We grudge her no achievement or distinction of learning or of pacific enterprise such as have made her record very bright and very enviable. We do not wish to injure her or to block in any way her legitimate influence or power. We do not wish to fight her either with arms or with hostile arrangements of trade if she is willing to associate herself with us and the other peace-loving nations of the world in covenants of justice and law and fair dealing. We wish her only to accept a place of equality among the peoples of the world, – the new world in which we now live, – instead of a place of mastery.

Neither do we presume to suggest to her any alteration or modification of her institutions. But it is necessary, we must frankly say, and necessary as a preliminary to any intelligent dealings with her on our part, that we should know whom her spokesmen speak for when they speak to us, whether for the Reichstag majority or for the military party and the men whose creed is imperial domination.

We have spoken now, surely, in terms too concrete to admit of any further doubt or question. An evident principle runs through the whole program I have outlined. It is the principle of justice to all peoples and nationalities, and their right to live on equal terms of liberty and safety with one another, whether they be strong or weak. Unless this principle be made its foundation no part of the structure of international justice can stand. The people of the United States could act upon no other principle; and to the vindication of this principle they are ready to devote their lives, their honor, and everything that they possess. The moral climax of this the culminating and final war for human liberty has come, and they are ready to put their own strength, their own highest purpose, their own integrity and devotion to the test.

'The Fourteen Points Speech: Address Delivered at a Joint Session of the Two Houses of Congress, January 8, 1918.' *The Public Papers of Woodrow Wilson: War and Peace*, ed. Ray Stannard Baker and William E. Dodd (2 vols., New York, 1927), I, pp. 155-62

2   The United States defines the Terms for an Armistice, October 23, 1918

Military reverses in the late summer and early fall of 1918 convinced German leaders that the war was lost. A new government under Prince Max of Baden approached Wilson through Swiss intermediaries for an armistice. Secretary Lansing spelled out the American position in his message of October 23, 1918.

I have the honor to acknowledge the receipt of your note of the twenty-second transmitting a communication under date of the twentieth from the German Government and to advise you that the President has instructed me to reply thereto as follows:

'Having received the solemn and explicit assurance of the German Government that it unreservedly accepts the terms of peace laid down in his address to the Congress of the United States on the eighth of January, 1918, and the principles of settlement enunciated in his subsequent addresses, particularly the address of the twenty-seventh of September, and that it desires to discuss the details of their application, and that this wish and purpose emanate, not from those who have hitherto dictated German policy and conducted the present war on Germany's behalf, but from ministers who speak for the majority of the Reichstag and for an overwhelming majority of the German people; and having received also the explicit promise of the present German Government that the humane rules of civilized warfare will be observed both on land and sea by the German armed forces, the President of the United States feels that he cannot decline to take up with the Governments with which the Government of the United States is associated the question of an armistice.

'He deems it his duty to say again, however, that the only armistice he would feel justified in submitting for consideration would be one which should leave the United States and the powers associated with her in a position to enforce any arrangements that may be entered into and to make a renewal of hostilities on the part of Germany impossible. The President has, therefore, transmitted his correspondence with the present German authorities to the Governments with which the Government of the United States is associated as a belligerent, with the suggestion that, if those Governments are disposed to effect peace upon the terms and principles indicated, their military advisers and the military advisers of the United States be asked to submit to the Governments associated against Germany the necessary terms of such an armistice as will fully protect the interests of the peoples involved and insure to the associated Governments the unrestricted power to safeguard and enforce the details of the peace to which the German Government has agreed, provided they deem such an armistice possible from the military point of view. Should such terms of armistice be suggested, their acceptance by Germany will afford the best concrete evidence of her unequivocal acceptance of the terms and principles of peace from which the whole action proceeds.

'The President would deem himself lacking in candor did he not point out in the frankest possible terms the reason why extraordinary safeguards must be demanded. Significant and important as the constitutional changes seem to be which are spoken of by the German Foreign Secretary in his note of the twentieth of October, it does not appear that the principle of a government responsible to the German people has yet been fully worked out or that any guarantees either exist or are in contemplation that the alterations of principle and of practice now partially agreed upon will be permanent. Moreover, it does not appear that the heart of the present difficulty has been reached. It may be that future wars have been brought under the control of the German people, but the present war has not been; and it is with the present war that we are dealing. It is evident that the German people have no means of commanding the acquiescence of the military authorities of the Empire in the popular will; that the power of the King of Prussia to control the policy of the Empire is unimpaired; that the determining initiative still remains with those who have hitherto been the masters of Germany.

'Feeling that the whole peace of the world depends now on plain speaking and straightforward action, the President deems it his duty to say, without any attempt to soften what may seem harsh words, that the nations of the world do not and cannot trust the word of those who have hitherto been the masters of German policy, and to point out once more that in concluding peace and attempting to undo the infinite injuries and injustices of this war the Government of the United States cannot deal with any but veritable representatives of the German people who have been assured of a genuine constitutional standing as the real rulers of Germany. If it must deal with the military masters and the monarchical autocrats of Germany now, or if it is likely to have to deal with them later in regard to the international obligations of the German Empire, it must demand, not peace negotiations, but s urrender. Nothing can be gained by leaving this essential thing unsaid.'

Secretary Lansing to the Imperial German Government, October 23, 1918, State Department Archives

3   President Wilson explains American Goals on the Eve of the Paris Conference, December 28, 1918

The armistice was signed on November 11, 1918. Wilson sailed for Europe three weeks later. On the eve of the opening of the Paris Peace Conference, the President offered his views on a 'new world order' in an address in London.

MR. LORD MAYOR:

We have come upon times when ceremonies like this have a new significance, and it is that significance which most impresses me as I stand here. The address which I have just heard is most generously and graciously conceived and the delightful accent of sincerity in it seems like a part of that voice of counsel which is now everywhere to be heard.

I feel that a distinguished honor has been conferred upon me by this reception, and I beg to assure you, sir, and your associates of my very profound appreciation, but I know that I am only part of what I may call a great body of circumstances. I do not believe that it was fancy on my part that I heard in the voice of welcome uttered in the streets of this great city and in the streets of Paris something more than a personal welcome. It seemed to me that I heard the voice of one people speaking to another people, and it was a voice in which one could distinguish a singular combination of emotions. There was surely there the deep gratefulness that the fighting was over. There was the pride that the fighting had had such a culmination. There was that sort of gratitude that the nations engaged had produced such men as the soldiers of Great Britain and of the United States and of France and of Italy – men whose prowess and achievements they had witnessed with rising admiration as they moved from culmination to culmination. But there was something more in it, the consciousness that the business is not yet done, the consciousness that it now rests upon others to see that those lives were not lost in vain.

I have not yet been to the actual battlefields, but I have been with many of the men who have fought the battles, and the other day I had the pleasure of being present at a session of the French Academy when they admitted Marshal Joffre to their membership. The sturdy, serene soldier stood and uttered, not the words of triumph, but the simple words of affection for his soldiers, and the conviction which he summed up, in a sentence which I will not try accurately to quote but reproduce in its spirit, was that France must always remember that the small and the weak could never live free in the world unless the strong and the great always put their power and strength in the service of right. That is the afterthought – the thought that something must be done now not only to make the just settlements, that of course, but to see that the settlements remained and were observed and that honor and justice prevailed in the world. And as I have conversed with the soldiers, I have been more and more aware that they fought for something that not all of them had defined, but which all of them recognized the moment you stated it to them. They fought to do away with an old order and to establish a new one, and the center and characteristic of the old order was that unstable thing which we used to call the 'balance of power' – a thing in which the balance was determined by the sword which was thrown in the one side or the other; a balance which was determined by the unstable equilibrium of competitive interests; a balance which was maintained by jealous watchfulness and an antagonism of interests which, though it was generally latent, was always deep-seated. The men who have fought in this war have been the men from free nations who were determined that that sort of thing should end now and forever.

It is very interesting to me to observe how from every quarter, from every sort of mind, from every concert of counsel, there comes the suggestion that there must now be, not a balance of power, not one powerful group of nations set off against another, but a single overwhelming, powerful group of nations who shall be the trustee of the peace of the world. It has been delightful in my conferences with the leaders of your Government to find how our minds moved along exactly the same line, and how our thought was always that the key to the peace was the guarantee of the peace, not the items of it; that the items would be worthless unless there stood back of them a permanent concert of power for their maintenance. That is the most reassuring thing that has ever happened in the world. When this war began the thought of a League of Nations was indulgently considered as the interesting thought of closeted students. It was thought of as one of those things that it was right to characterize by a name which as a university man I have always resented; it was said to be academic, as if that in itself were a condemnation, something that men could think about but never get. Now we find the practical leading minds of the world determined to get it. No such sudden and potent union of purpose has ever been witnessed in the world before. Do you wonder, therefore, gentlemen, that in common with those who represent you I am eager to get at the business and write the sentences down; and that

I am particularly happy that the ground is cleared and the foundations laid – for we have already accepted the same body of principles? Those principles are clearly and definitely enough stated to make their application a matter which should afford no fundamental difficulty. And back of us is that imperative yearning of the world to have all disturbing questions quieted, to have all threats against peace silenced, to have just men everywhere come together for a common object. The peoples of the world want peace and they want it now, not merely by conquest of arms, but by agreement of mind.

It was this incomparably great object that brought me overseas. It has never before been deemed excusable for a President of the United States to leave the territory of the United States; but I know that I have the support of the judgment of my colleagues in the Government of the United States in saying that it was my paramount duty to turn away even from the imperative tasks at home to lend such counsel and aid as I could to this great, may I not say, final enterprise of humanity.

> 'At the Guild Hall, London: Response to an Address of Welcome by the Lord Mayor, December 28, 1918.' *The Public Papers of Woodrow Wilson: War and Peace*, ed. Ray Stannard Baker and William E. Dodd (2 vols., New York, 1927), I, pp. 341-4

4   President Wilson on the League of Nations, January 25, 1919

The establishment of a League of Nations was central to Wilson's peace programme. The second Plenary Session voted on January 25 to include the League in the peace settlement after hearing the following address by the American President.

MR. CHAIRMAN:

I consider it a distinguished privilege to be permitted to open the discussion in this conference on the League of Nations. We have assembled for two purposes, to make the present settlements which have been rendered necessary by this war, and also to secure the peace of the world, not only by the present settlements, but by the arrangements we shall make at this conference for its maintenance. The League of Nations seems to me to be necessary for both of these purposes. There are many complicated questions connected with the present settlements which perhaps cannot be successfully worked out to an ultimate issue by the decisions we shall arrive at here. I can easily conceive that many of these settlements will need subsequent reconsideration, that many of the decisions we make shall need subsequent alteration in some degree; for, if I may judge by my own study of some of these questions, they are not susceptible of confident judgments at present.

It is, therefore, necessary that we should set up some machinery by which the work of this conference should be rendered complete. We have assembled here for the purpose of doing very much more than making the present settlements. We are assembled under very peculiar conditions of world opinion. I may say without straining the point that we are not representatives of Governments, but representatives of peoples. It will not suffice to satisfy governmental circles anywhere. It is necessary that we should satisfy the opinion of mankind. The burdens of this war have fallen in an unusual degree upon the whole population of the countries involved. I do not need to draw for you the picture of how the burden has been thrown back from the front upon the older men, upon the women, upon the children, upon the homes of the civilized world, and how the real strain of the war has come where the eye of government could not reach, but where the heart of humanity beats. We are bidden by these people to make a peace which will make them secure. We are bidden by these people to see to it that this strain does not come upon them again, and I venture to say that it has been possible for them to bear this strain because they hoped that those who represented them could get together after this war and make such another sacrifice unnecessary.

It is a solemn obligation on our part, therefore, to make permanent arrangements that justice shall be rendered and peace maintained. This is the central object of our meeting. Settlements may be temporary, but the action of the nations in the interest of peace and justice must be permanent. We can set up permanent processes. We may not be able to set up permanent decisions. Therefore, it seems to me that we must take, so far as we can, a picture of the world into our minds. Is it not a startling circumstance, for one thing, that the great discoveries of science, that the quiet studies of men in laboratories, that the thoughtful developments which have taken place in quiet lecture rooms, have now been turned to the destruction of civilization? The powers of destruction have not so much multiplied as gained facility. The enemy whom we have just overcome had at his seats of learning some of the principal centers of scientific study and discovery, and he used them in order to make destruction sudden and complete; and only the watchful, continuous coöperation of men can see to it that science as well as armed men is kept within the harness of civilization.

In a sense the United States is less interested in this subject than the other nations here assembled. With her great territory and her extensive sea borders, it is less likely that the United States should suffer from the attack of enemies than that many of the other nations here should suffer; and the ardor of the United States – for it is a very deep and genuine ardor – for the society of nations is not an ardor springing out of fear or apprehension, but an ardor springing out of the ideals which have come to consciousness in this war. In coming into this war the United States never for a moment thought that she was intervening in the politics of Europe or the politics of Asia or the politics of any part of the world. Her thought was that all the world had now become conscious that there was a single cause which turned upon the issues of this war. That was the cause of justice and of liberty for men of every kind and place. Therefore, the United States should feel that its part in this war had been played in vain if there ensued upon it merely a body of European settlements. It would feel that it could not take part in guaranteeing those European settlements unless that guarantee involved the continuous superintendence of the peace of the world by the associated nations of the world.

Therefore, it seems to me that we must concert our best judgment in order to make this League of Nations a vital thing – not merely a formal thing, not an occasional thing, not a thing sometimes called into life to meet an exigency, but always functioning in watchful attendance upon the interests of the nations – and that its continuity should be a vital continuity; that it should have functions that are continuing functions and that do not permit an intermission of its watchfulness and of its labor; that it should be the eye of the nations to keep watch upon the common interest, an eye that does not slumber, an eye that is everywhere watchful and attentive.

And if we do not make it vital, what shall we do? We shall disappoint the expectations of the peoples. This is what their thought centers upon. I have had the very delightful experience of visiting several nations since I came to this side of the water, and every time the voice of the body of the people reached me through any representative, at the front of its plea stood the hope for the League of Nations. Gentlemen, the select classes of mankind are no longer the governors of mankind. The fortunes of mankind are now in the hands of the plain people of the whole world. Satisfy them, and you have justified their confidence not only, but established peace. Fail to satisfy them, and no arrangement that you can make will either set up or steady the peace of the world.

You can imagine, gentlemen, I dare say, the sentiments and the purpose with which representatives of the United States support this great project for a League of Nations. We regard it as the keystone of the whole program which expressed our purposes and ideals in this war and which the associated nations have accepted as the basis of the settlement. If we returned to the United States without having made every effort in our power to realize this program, we should return to meet the merited scorn of our fellow citizens. For they are a body that constitutes a great democracy. They expect their leaders to speak their thoughts and no private purpose of their own. They expect their representatives to be their servants. We have no choice but to obey their mandate. But it is with the greatest enthusiasm and pleasure that we accept that mandate; and because this is the keystone of the whole fabric, we have pledged our every purpose to it, as we have to every item of the fabric. We would not dare abate a single part of the program which constitutes our instruction. We would not dare compromise upon any matter as the champion of this thing – this peace of the world, this attitude of justice, this principle that we are the masters of no people but are here to see that every people in the world shall choose its own masters and govern its own destinies, not as we wish, but as it wishes. We are here to see, in short, that the very foundations of this war are swept away. Those foundations were the private choice of small coteries of civil rulers and military staffs. Those foundations were the aggression of great powers upon the small. Those foundations were the holding together of empires of unwilling subjects by the duress of arms. Those foundations were the power of small bodies of men to work their will upon mankind and use them as pawns in a game. And nothing less than the emancipation of the world from these things will accomplish peace. You can see that the representatives of the United States are, therefore, never put to the embarrassment of choosing a way of expediency, because they have laid down for them the unalterable lines of principle. And, thank God, those lines have been accepted as the lines of settlement by all the high-minded men who have had to do with the beginnings of this great business.

I hope, Mr. Chairman, that when it is known, as I feel confident it will be known, that we have adopted the principle of the League of Nations and mean to work out that principle in effective action, we shall by that single thing have lifted a great part of the load of anxiety from the hearts of men everywhere. We stand in a peculiar case. As I go about the streets here I see everywhere the American uniform. Those men came into the war after we had uttered our purposes.

They came as crusaders, not merely to win a war, but to win a cause; and I am responsible to them, for it fell to me to formulate the purposes for which I asked them to fight, and I, like them, must be a crusader for these things, whatever it costs and whatever it may be necessary to do, in honor, to accomplish the object for which they fought. I have been glad to find from day to day that there is no question of our standing alone in this matter, for there are champions of this cause upon every hand. I am merely avowing this in order that you may understand why, perhaps, it fell to us, who are disengaged from the politics of this great continent and of the Orient, to suggest that this was the keystone of the arch, and why it occurred to the generous mind of our president to call upon me to open this debate. It is not because we alone represent this idea, but because it is our privilege to associate ourselves with you in representing it.

I have only tried in what I have said to give you the fountains of the enthusiasm which is within us for this thing, for those fountains spring, it seems to me, from all the ancient wrongs and sympathies of mankind, and the very pulse of the world seems to beat to the surface in this enterprise.

> 'Make This League of Nations a Vital Thing: Address Before the Second Plenary Session of the Peace Conference, Paris, January 25, 1919.' *The Public Papers of Woodrow Wilson: War and Peace*, ed. Ray Stannard Baker and William E. Dodd (2 vols., New York, 1927), I, pp. 395-400

5 Article X of the Covenant

If the League was vital for the maintenance of peace in the world, Article X, Wilson stated on many occasions, was 'the heart of the Covenant'.

Article X

The High Contracting Parties undertake to respect and preserve as against external aggression the territorial integrity and existing political independence of all States members of the League. In case of any such aggression or in case of any threat or danger of such aggression the Executive Council shall advise upon the means by which this obligation shall be fulfilled.

6 Senator Lodge opposes the Treaty, August 12, 1919

Henry Cabot Lodge of Massachusetts led the fight in the Senate against the Paris settlement. Among the numerous statements detailing his disapproval, his speech of August 12, 1919, was typical.

. . . Never forget that this league is primarily – I might say overwhelmingly – a political organization, and I object strongly to having the politics of the United States turn upon disputes where deep feeling is aroused but in which we have no direct interest. It will all tend to delay the Americanization of our great population, and it is more important not only to the United States but to the peace of the world to make all these people good Americans than it is to determine that some piece of territory should belong to one European country rather than to another. For this reason I wish to limit strictly our interference in the affairs of Europe and of Africa. We have interests of our own in Asia and in the Pacific which we must guard upon our own account, but the less we undertake to play the part of umpire and thrust ourselves into European conflicts the better for the United States and for the world.

It has been reiterated here on this floor, and reiterated to the point of weariness, that in every treaty there is some sacrifice of sovereignty. That is not a universal truth by any means, but it is true of some treaties and it is a platitude which does not require reiteration. The question and the only question before us here is how much of our sovereignty we are justified in sacrificing. In what I have already said about other nations putting us into war I have covered one point of sovereignty which ought never to be yielded – the power to send American soldiers and sailors everywhere, which ought never to be taken from the American people or impaired in the slightest degree. Let us beware how we palter with our independence. We have not reached the great position from which we were able to come down into the field of battle and help to save the world from tyranny by being guided by others. Our vast power has all been built up and gathered together by ourselves alone. We forced our way upward from the days of the Revolution, through a world often hostile and always indifferent. We owe no debt to anyone except to France in that Revolution, and those policies and those rights on which our power has been founded should never be lessened or weakened. It will be no service to the world to do so and it will be of intolerable injury to the United States. We will do our share. We are ready and anxious to help in all ways to preserve the world's peace. But we can do it best by not crippling ourselves.

I am as anxious as any human being can be to have the United States render every possible service to the civilization and the peace of mankind, but I am certain we can do it best by not putting ourselves in leading strings or subjecting our policies and our sovereignty to other nations. The independence of the United States is not only more precious to ourselves but to the world than any single possession. Look at the United States to-day. We have made mistakes in the past. We have had shortcomings. We shall make mistakes in the future and fall short of our own best hopes. But none the less is there any country to-day on the face of the earth which can compare with this in ordered liberty, in peace, and in the largest freedom? I feel that I can say this without being accused of undue boastfulness, for it is the simple fact, and in making this treaty and taking on these obligations all that we do is in a spirit of unselfishness and in a desire for the good of mankind. But it is well to remember that we are dealing with nations every one of which has a direct individual interest to serve, and there is grave danger in an unshared idealism. Contrast the United States with any country on the face of the earth to-day and ask yourself whether the situation of the United States is not the best to be found. I will go as far as anyone in world service, but the first step to world service is the maintenance of the United States. You may call me selfish, if you will, conservative or reactionary, or use any other harsh adjective you see fit to apply, but an American I was born, an American I have remained all my life. I can never be anything else but an American, and I must think of the United States first, and when I think of the United States first in an arrangement like this I am thinking of what is best for the world, for if the United States fails the best hopes of mankind fail with it. I have never had but one allegiance – I can not divide it now. I have loved but one flag and I can not share that devotion and give affection to the mongrel banner invented for a league. Internationalism, illustrated by the Bolshevik and by the men to whom all countries are alike provided they can make money out of them, is to me repulsive. National I must remain, and in that way I like all other Americans can render the amplest service to the world. The United States is the world's best hope, but if you fetter her in the interests and quarrels of other nations, if you tangle her in the intrigues of Europe, you will destroy her power for good and endanger her very existence. Leave her to march freely through the centuries to come as in the years that have gone. Strong, generous, and confident, she has nobly served mankind. Beware how you trifle with your marvelous inheritance, this great land of ordered liberty, for if we stumble and fall freedom and civilization everywhere will go down in ruin.

We are told that we shall 'break the heart of the world' if we do not take this league just as it stands. I fear that the hearts of the vast majority of mankind would beat on strongly and steadily and without any quickening if the league were to perish altogether. If it should be effectively and beneficiently changed the people who would lie awake in sorrow for a single night could be easily gathered in one not very large room but those who would draw a long breath of relief would reach to millions.

We hear much of visions and I trust we shall continue to have visions and dream dreams of a fairer future for the race. But visions are one thing and visionaries are another, and the mechanical appliances of the rhetorician designed to give a picture of a present which does not exist and of a future which no man can predict are as unreal and short lived as the steam or canvas clouds, the angels suspended on wires and the artificial lights of the stage. They pass with the moment of effect and are shabby and tawdry in the daylight. Let us at least be real. Washington's entire honesty of mind and his fearless look into the face of all facts are qualities which can never go out of fashion and which we should all do well to imitate.

Ideals have been thrust upon us as an argument for the league until the healthy mind which rejects cant revolts from them. Are ideals confined to this deformed experiment upon a noble purpose, tainted, as it is, with bargains and tied to a peace treaty which might have been disposed of long ago to the great benefit of the world if it had not been compelled to carry this rider on its back? 'Post equitem sedet atra cura', Horace tells us, but no blacker care ever sat behind any rider than we shall find in this covenant of doubtful and disputed interpretation as it now perches upon the treaty of peace.

No doubt many excellent and patriotic people see a coming fulfilment of noble ideals in the words 'League for Peace'. We all respect and share these aspirations and desires, but some of us see no hope, but rather defeat, for them in this murky covenant. For we, too, have our ideals, even if we differ from those who have tried to establish a monopoly of idealism. Our first ideal is our country, and we see her in the future, as in the past, giving service to all her people and to the world. Our ideal of the future is that she should continue to render that service of her own free will. She has great problems of her own to solve, very grim and perilous problems, and a right solution, if we can attain to it, would largely benefit mankind. We would have our country strong to resist a peril from the West, as she has flung back the German menace from the East. We would not have our politics distracted and embittered by the dissensions of other lands. We would not have our country's vigor exhausted, or her moral force abated, by everlasting meddling and muddling in every quarrel, great and small, which afflicts the world. Our ideal is to make her ever stronger and better and finer, because in that way alone, as we believe, can she be of the greatest service to the world's peace and to the welfare of mankind. [Prolonged applause in the galleries.]

Congressional Record, 66th Congress, 1st Session (August 12, 1919), p. 3784

7   President Wilson on the Meaning of the Peace Settlement, September 25, 1919

Wilson's swing through the West in the late summer of 1919 represented a massive effort to mobilize public opinion behind the Treaty. The President poured out his heart to the American people, but to no avail. The personal cost to Wilson was also high. He collapsed on September 26, the day following his speech at Pueblo, never to regain full health.

At Pueblo, Colo., September 25, 1919.

MR. CHAIRMAN AND FELLOW COUNTRYMEN:
    It is with a great deal of genuine pleasure that I find myself in Pueblo, and I feel it a compliment that I should be permitted to be the first speaker in this beautiful hall. One of the advantages of this hall, as I look about, is that you are not too far away from me, because there is nothing so reassuring to men who are trying to express the public sentiment as getting into real personal contact with their fellow citizens. I have gained a renewed impression as I have crossed the continent this time of the homogeneity of this great people to whom we belong. They come from many stocks, but they are all of one kind. They come from many origins, but they are all shot through with the same principles and desire the same righteous and honest things. I have received a more inspiring impression this time of the public opinion of the United States than it was ever my privilege to receive before.
    The chief pleasure of my trip has been that it has nothing to do with

my personal fortunes, that it has nothing to do with my personal reputation, that it has nothing to do with anything except great principles uttered by Americans of all sorts and of all parties which we are now trying to realize at this crisis of the affairs of the world. But there have been unpleasant impressions as well as pleasant impressions, my fellow citizens, as I have crossed the continent. I have perceived more and more that men have been busy creating an absolutely false impression of what the treaty of peace and the Covenant of the League of Nations contain and mean. I find, moreover, that there is an organized propaganda against the League of Nations and against the treaty proceeding from exactly the same sources that the organized propaganda proceeded from which threatened this country here and there with disloyalty, and I want to say – I cannot say too often – any man who carries a hyphen about with him carries a dagger that he is ready to plunge into the vitals of this Republic whenever he gets ready. If I can catch any man with a hyphen in this great contest I will know that I have got an enemy of the Republic. My fellow citizens, it is only certain bodies of foreign sympathies, certain bodies of sympathy with foreign nations that are organized against this great document which the American representatives have brought back from Paris. Therefore, in order to clear away the mists, in order to remove the impressions, in order to check the falsehoods that have clustered around this great subject, I want to tell you a few very simple things about the treaty and the Covenant.

Do not think of this treaty of peace as merely a settlement with Germany. It is that. It is a very severe settlement with Germany, but there is not anything in it that she did not earn. Indeed, she earned more than she can ever be able to pay for, and the punishment exacted of her is not a punishment greater than she can bear, and it is absolutely necessary in order that no other nation may ever plot such a thing against humanity and civilization. But the treaty is so much more than that. It is not merely a settlement with Germany; it is a readjustment of those great injustices which underlie the whole structure of European and Asiatic society. This is only the first of several treaties. They are all constructed upon the same plan. The Austrian treaty follows the same lines. The treaty with Hungary follows the same lines. The treaty with Bulgaria follows the same lines. The treaty with Turkey, when it is formulated, will follow the same lines. What are those lines? They are based upon the purpose to see that every government dealt with in this great settlement is put in the hands of the people and taken out of the hands of coteries and of sovereigns who had no right to rule over the people. It is a people's treaty, that accomplishes by a great sweep of practical justice the liberation of men who never could have liberated themselves, and the power of the most powerful nations has been devoted not to their aggrandizement but to the liberation of people whom they could have put under their control if they had chosen to do so. Not one foot of territory is demanded by the conquerors, not one single item of submission to their authority is demanded by them. The men who sat around that table in Paris knew that the time had come when the people were no longer going to consent to live under masters, but were going to live the lives that they chose themselves, to live under such governments as they chose themselves to erect. That is the fundamental principle of this great settlement.

And we did not stop with that. We added a great international charter for the rights of labor. Reject this treaty, impair it, and this is the consequence to the laboring men of the world, that there is no international tribunal which can bring the moral judgments of the world to bear upon the great labor questions of the day. What we need to do with regard to the labor questions of the day, my fellow countrymen, is to lift them into the light, is to lift them out of the haze and distraction of passion, of hostility, not into the calm spaces where men look at things without passion. The more men you get into a great discussion the more you exclude passion. Just so soon as the calm judgment of the world is directed upon the question of justice to labor, labor is going to have a forum such as it never was supplied with before, and men everywhere are going to see that the problem of labor is nothing more nor less than the problem of the elevation of humanity. We must see that all the questions which have disturbed the world, all the questions which have eaten into the confidence of men toward their governments, all the questions which have disturbed the processes of industry, shall be brought out where men of all points of view, men of all attitudes of mind, men of all kinds of experience, may contribute their part to the settlement of the great questions which we must settle and cannot ignore.

At the front of this great treaty is put the Covenant of the League of Nations. It will also be at the front of the Austrian treaty and the Hungarian treaty and the Bulgarian treaty and the treaty with Turkey. Every one of them will contain the Covenant of the League of Nations, because you cannot work any of them without the Covenant of the League of Nations. Unless you get the united, concerted purpose and power of the great Governments of the world behind this settlement, it will fall down like a house of cards. There is only one power to put behind the liberation of mankind, and that is the power of mankind. It is the power of the united moral forces of the world, and in the Covenant of the League of Nations the moral forces of the world are mobilized. For what purpose? Reflect, my fellow citizens, that the membership of this great League is going to include all the great fighting nations of the world, as well as the weak ones. It is not for the present going to include Germany, but for the time being Germany is not a great fighting country. All the nations that have power that can be mobilized are going to be members of this League, including the United States. And what do they unite for? They enter into a solemn promise to one another that they will never use their power against one another for aggression; that they never will impair the territorial integrity of a neighbor; that they never will interfere with the political independence of a neighbor; that they will abide by the principle that great populations are entitled to determine their own destiny and that they will not interfere with that destiny; and that no matter what differences arise amongst them they will never resort to war without first having done one or other of two things – either submitted the matter of controversy to arbitration, in which case they agree to abide by the result without question, or submitted it to the consideration of the council of the League of Nations, laying before that council all the documents, all the facts, agreeing that the council can publish the documents and the facts to the whole world, agreeing that there shall be six months allowed for the mature consideration of those facts by the council, and agreeing that at the expiration of the six months, even if they are not then ready to accept the advice of the council with regard to the settlement of the dispute, they will still not go to war for another three months. In other words, they consent, no matter what happens, to submit every matter of difference between them to the judgment of mankind, and just so certainly as they do that, my fellow citizens, war will be in the far background, war will be pushed out of that foreground of terror in which it has kept the world for generation after generation, and men will know that there will be a calm time of deliberate counsel. The most dangerous thing for a bad cause is to expose it to the opinion of the world. The most certain way that you can prove that a man is mistaken is by letting all his neighbors know what he thinks, by letting all his neighbors discuss what he thinks, and if he is in the wrong you will notice that he will stay at home, he will not walk on the street. He will be afraid of the eyes of his neighbors. He will be afraid of their judgment of his character. He will know that his cause is lost unless he can sustain it by the arguments

of right and of justice. The same law that applies to individuals applies
to nations.

But, you say, 'We have heard that we might be at a disadvantage in
the League of Nations'. Well, whoever told you that either was deliberately falsifying or he had not read the Covenant of the League of
Nations. I leave him the choice. I want to give you a very simple
account of the organization of the League of Nations and let you judge
for yourselves. It is a very simple organization. The power of the
League, or rather the activities of the League, lie in two bodies. There
is the council, which consists of one representative from each of the
principal allied and associated powers – that is to say, the United States,
Great Britain, France, Italy, and Japan, along with four other representatives of smaller powers chosen out of the general body of the
membership of the League. The council is the source of every active
policy of the League, and no active policy of the League can be adopted
without a unanimous vote of the council. That is explicitly stated in
the Covenant itself. Does it not evidently follow that the League of
Nations can adopt no policy whatever without the consent of the
United States? The affirmative vote of the representative of the United
States is necessary in every case. Now, you have heard of six votes
belonging to the British Empire. Those six votes are not in the council.
They are in the assembly, and the interesting thing is that the assembly
does not vote. I must qualify that statement a little, but essentially it is
absolutely true. In every matter in which the assembly is given a voice,
and there are only four or five, its vote does not count unless concurred
in by the representatives of all the nations represented on the council,
so that there is no validity to any vote of the assembly unless in that
vote also the representative of the United States concurs. That one vote
of the United States is as big as the six votes of the British Empire. I
am not jealous for advantage, my fellow citizens, but I think that is a
perfectly safe situation. There is no validity in a vote, either by the
council or the assembly, in which we do not concur. So much for the
statements about the six votes of the British Empire.

Look at it in another aspect. The assembly is the talking body. The
assembly was created in order that anybody that purposed anything
wrong should be subjected to the awkward circumstance that every-
body could talk about it. This is the great assembly in which all the
things that are likely to disturb the peace of the world or the good
understanding between nations are to be exposed to the general view,
and I want to ask you if you think it was unjust, unjust to the United
States, that speaking parts should be assigned to the several portions

of the British Empire? Do you think it unjust that there should be some spokesman in debate for that fine little stout Republic down in the Pacific, New Zealand? Do you think it was unjust that Australia should be allowed to stand up and take part in the debate – Australia, from which we have learned some of the most useful progressive policies of modern time, a little nation only five million in a great continent, but counting for several times five in its activities and in its interest in liberal reform? Do you think it unjust that that little Republic down in South Africa, whose gallant resistance to being subjected to any outside authority at all we admired for so many months and whose fortunes we followed with such interest, should have a speaking part? Great Britain obliged South Africa to submit to her sovereignty, but she immediately after that felt that it was convenient and right to hand the whole self-government of that colony over to the very men whom she had beaten. The representatives of South Africa in Paris were two of the most distinguished generals of the Boer Army, two of the realest men I ever met, two men that could talk sober counsel and wise advice, along with the best statesmen in Europe. To exclude General Botha and General Smuts from the right to stand up in the parliament of the world and say something concerning the affairs of mankind would be absurd. And what about Canada? Is not Canada a good neighbor? I ask you, Is not Canada more likely to agree with the United States than with Great Britain? Canada has a speaking part. And then, for the first time in the history of the world, that great voiceless multitude, that throng hundreds of millions strong in India, has a voice, and I want to testify that some of the wisest and most dignified figures in the peace conference at Paris came from India, men who seemed to carry in their minds an older wisdom than the rest of us had, whose traditions ran back into so many of the unhappy fortunes of mankind that they seemed very useful counselors as to how some ray of hope and some prospect of happiness could be opened to its people. I for my part have no jealousy whatever of those five speaking parts in the assembly. Those speaking parts cannot translate themselves into five votes that can in any matter override the voice and purpose of the United States.

Let us sweep aside all this language of jealousy. Let us be big enough to know the facts and to welcome the facts, because the facts are based upon the principle that America has always fought for, namely, the equality of self-governing peoples, whether they were big or little – not counting men, but counting rights, not counting representation, but counting the purpose of that representation. When you hear an opinion quoted you do not count the number of persons who hold it; you ask, 'Who said that?' You weigh opinions, you do not count them, and the beauty of all democracies is that every voice can be heard, every voice can have its effect, every voice can contribute to the general judgment that is finally arrived at. That is the object of democracy. Let us accept what America has always fought for, and accept it with pride that America showed the way and made the proposal. I do not mean that America made the proposal in this particular instance; I mean that the principle was an American principle, proposed by America.

When you come to the heart of the Covenant, my fellow citizens, you will find it in Article X, and I am very much interested to know that the other things have been blown away like bubbles. There is nothing in the other contentions with regard to the League of Nations, but there is something in Article X that you ought to realize and ought to accept or reject. Article X is the heart of the whole matter. What is Article X? I never am certain that I can from memory give a literal repetition of its language, but I am sure that I can give an exact inter- pretation of its meaning. Article X provides that every member of the League covenants to respect and preserve the territorial integrity and existing political independence of every other member of the League as against external aggression. Not against internal disturbance. There was not a man at that table who did not admit the sacredness of the right of self-determination, the sacredness of the right of any body of people to say that they would not continue to live under the Govern- ment they were then living under, and under Article XI of the Cove- nant they are given a place to say whether they will live under it or not. For following Article X is Article XI, which makes it the right of any member of the League at any time to call attention to anything, anywhere, that is likely to disturb the peace of the world or the good understanding between nations upon which the peace of the world depends. I want to give you an illustration of what that would mean.

You have heard a great deal – something that was true and a great deal that was false – about that provision of the treaty which hands over to Japan the rights which Germany enjoyed in the Province of Shantung in China. In the first place, Germany did not enjoy any rights there that other nations had not already claimed. For my part, my judgment, my moral judgment, is against the whole set of concessions. They were all of them unjust to China, they ought never to have been exacted, they were all exacted by duress, from a great body of thoughtful and ancient and helpless people. There never was any right in any of them. Thank God, America never asked for any, never dreamed of asking for any. But when Germany got this concession in 1898, the Government of the United States made no protest whatever. That was not because the Government of the United States was not in the hands of high-minded and conscientious men. It was. William McKinley was President and John Hay was Secretary of State – as safe hands to leave the honor of the United States in as any that you can cite. They made no protest because the state of international law at that time was that it was none of their business unless they could show that the interests of the United States were affected, and the only thing that they could show with regard to the interests of the United States was that Germany might close the doors of Shantung Province against the trade of the United States. They, therefore, demanded and obtained promises that we could continue to sell merchandise in Shantung. Immediately following that concession to Germany there was a concession to Russia of the same sort, of Port Arthur, and Port Arthur was handed over subsequently to Japan on the very territory of the United States. Don't you remember that when Russia and Japan got into war with one another the war was brought to a conclusion by a treaty written at Portsmouth, N. H., and in that treaty without the slightest intimation from any authoritative sources in America that the Government of the United States had any objection, Port Arthur, Chinese territory, was turned over to Japan? I want you distinctly to understand that there is no thought of criticism in my mind. I am expounding to you a state of international law. Now, read Articles X and XI. You will see that international law is revolutionized by putting morals into it. Article X says that no member of the League, and that includes all these nations that have demanded these things unjustly of China, shall impair the territorial integrity or the political independence of any other member of the League. China is going to be a member of the League. Article XI says that any member of the League can call attention to anything that is likely to disturb the peace of the world or the good understanding between nations, and China is for the first time in the history of mankind afforded a standing before the jury of the world. I, for my part, have a profound sympathy for China, and I am proud to have taken part in an arrangement which promises the protection of the world to the rights of China. The whole atmosphere of the world is changed by a thing like that, my fellow citizens. The whole international practice of the world is revolutionized.

But you will say, 'What is the second sentence of Article X? That is what gives very disturbing thoughts.' The second sentence is that the council of the League shall advise what steps, if any, are necessary to carry out the guarantee of the first sentence, namely, that the members will respect and preserve the territorial integrity and political independence of the other members. I do not know any other meaning for the word 'advise' except 'advise'. The council advises, and it cannot advise without the vote of the United States. Why gentlemen should fear that the Congress of the United States would be advised to do something that it did not want to do I frankly cannot imagine, because they cannot even be advised to do anything unless their own representative has participated in the advice. It may be that that will impair somewhat the vigor of the League, but, nevertheless, the fact is so, that we are not obliged to take any advice except our own, which to any man who wants to go his own course is a very satisfactory state of affairs. Every man regards his own advice as best, and I dare say every man mixes his own advice with some thought of his own interest. Whether we use it wisely or unwisely, we can use the vote of the United States to make impossible drawing the United States into any enterprise that she does not care to be drawn into.

Yet Article X strikes at the taproot of war. Article X is a statement that the very things that have always been sought in imperialistic wars are henceforth forgone by every ambitious nation in the world. I would have felt very lonely, my fellow countrymen, and I would have felt very much disturbed if, sitting at the peace table in Paris, I had supposed that I was expounding my own ideas. Whether you believe it or not, I know the relative size of my own ideas; I know how they stand related in bulk and proportion to the moral judgments of my fellow countrymen, and I proposed nothing whatever at the peace table at Paris that I had not sufficiently certain knowledge embodied the moral judgment of the citizens of the United States. I had gone over there with, so to say, explicit instructions. Don't you remember that we laid down fourteen points which should contain the principles of the settlement? They were not my points. In every one of them I was conscientiously trying to read the thought of the people of the United States, and after I uttered those points I had every assurance given me that could be given me that they did speak the moral judgment of the United States and not my single judgment. Then when it came to that critical period just a little less than a year ago, when it was evident that the war was coming to its critical end, all the nations engaged in the war accepted those fourteen principles explicitly as the basis of the armistice and the basis of the peace. In those circumstances I crossed the ocean under bond to my own people and to the other governments with which I was dealing. The whole specification of the method of settlement was written down and accepted beforehand, and we were architects building on those specifications. It reassures me and fortifies my position to find how before I went over men whose judgment the United States has often trusted were of exactly the same opinion that I went abroad to express. Here is something I want to read from Theodore Roosevelt:

'The one effective move for obtaining peace is by an agreement among all the great powers in which each should pledge itself not only to abide by the decisions of a common tribunal but to back its decisions by force. The great civilized nations should combine by solemn agreement in a great world league for the peace of righteousness; a court should be established. A changed and amplified Hague court would meet the requirements, composed of representatives from each nation, whose representatives are sworn to act as judges in each case and not in a representative capacity.' Now there is Article X. He goes on and says this: 'The nations should agree on certain rights that should not be questioned, such as territorial integrity, their right to deal with their domestic affairs, and with such matters as whom they should admit to citizenship. All such guarantee each of their number in possession of these rights.'

Now, the other specification is in the Covenant. The Covenant in another portion guarantees to the members the independent control of their domestic questions. There is not a leg for these gentlemen to stand on when they say that the interests of the United States are not safe-guarded in the very points where we are most sensitive. You do not need to be told again that the Covenant expressly says that nothing in this Covenant shall be construed as affecting the validity of the Monroe Doctrine, for example. You could not be more explicit than that. And every point of interest is covered, partly for one very interesting reason. This is not the first time that the Foreign Relations Committee of the Senate of the United States has read and considered this Covenant. I brought it to this country in March last in a tentative, provisional form, in practically the form that it now has, with the exception of certain additions which I shall mention immediately. I asked the Foreign Relations Committees of both Houses to come to the White House and we spent a long evening in the frankest discussion of every portion that they wished to discuss. They made certain specific suggestions as to what should be contained in this document when it was to be revised. I carried those suggestions to Paris, and every one of them was adopted. What more could I have done? What more could have been obtained? The very matters upon which these gentlemen were most concerned were, the right of withdrawal, which is now expressly stated; the safeguarding of the Monroe Doctrine, which is now accomplished; the exclusion from action by the League of domestic questions, which is now accomplished. All along the line, every suggestion of the United States was adopted after the Covenant had been drawn up in its first form and had been published for the criticism of the world. There is a very true sense in which I can say this is a tested American document.

I am dwelling upon these points, my fellow citizens, in spite of the fact that I dare say to most of you they are perfectly well known, because in order to meet the present situation we have got to know what we are dealing with. We are not dealing with the kind of document which this is represented by some gentlemen to be; and inasmuch as we are dealing with a document simon-pure in respect of the very principles we have professed and lived up to, we have got to do one or other of two things – we have got to adopt it or reject it. There is no middle course. You cannot go in on a special-privilege basis of your own. I take it that you are too proud to ask to be exempted from responsibilities which the other members of the League will carry. We go in upon equal terms or we do not go in at all; and if we do not go in, my fellow citizens, think of the tragedy of that result – the only sufficient guarantee to the peace of the world withheld! Ourselves drawn apart with that dangerous pride which means that we shall be ready to take care of ourselves, and that means that we shall maintain great standing armies and an irresistible navy; that means we shall have the organization of a military nation; that means we shall have a general staff, with the kind of power that the general staff of Germany had; to mobilize this great manhood of the Nation when it pleases, all the energy of our young men drawn into the thought and preparation for war. What of our pledges to the men that lie dead in France? We said that they went over there not to prove the prowess of America or her readiness for another war but to see to it that there never was such a war again. It always seems to make it difficult for me to say anything, my fellow citizens, when I think of my clients in this case. My clients are the children; my clients are the next generation. They do not know what promises and bonds I undertook when I ordered the armies of the United States to the soil of France, but I know, and I intend to redeem my pledges to the children; they shall not be sent upon a similar errand.

Again and again, my fellow citizens, mothers who lost their sons in

France have come to me and, taking my hand, have shed tears upon it not only, but they have added, 'God bless you, Mr. President!' Why, my fellow citizens, should they pray God to bless me? I advised the Congress of the United States to create the situation that led to the death of their sons. I ordered their sons oversea. I consented to their sons being put in the most difficult parts of the battle line, where death was certain, as in the impenetrable difficulties of the forest of Argonne. Why should they weep upon my hand and call down the blessings of God upon me? Because they believe that their boys died for something that vastly transcends any of the immediate and palpable objects of the war. They believe, and they rightly believe, that their sons saved the liberty of the world. They believe that wrapped up with the liberty of the world is the continuous protection of that liberty by the concerted powers of all civilized people. They believe that this sacrifice was made in order that other sons should not be called upon for a similar gift – the gift of life, the gift of all that died – and if we did not see this thing through, if we fulfilled the dearest present wish of Germany and now dissociated ourselves from those alongside whom we fought in the war, would not something of the halo go away from the gun over the mantelpiece, or the sword? Would not the old uniform lose something of its significance? These men were crusaders. They were not going forth to prove the might of the United States. They were going forth to prove the might of justice and right, and all the world accepted them as crusaders, and their transcendent achievement has made all the world believe in America as it believes in no other nation organized in the modern world. There seems to me to stand between us and the rejection or qualification of this treaty the serried ranks of those boys in khaki, not only these boys who came home, but those dear ghosts that still deploy upon the fields of France.

My friends, on last Decoration Day I went to a beautiful hillside near Paris, where was located the cemetery of Suresnes, a cemetery given over to the burial of the American dead. Behind me on the slopes was rank upon rank of living American soldiers, and lying before me upon the levels of the plain was rank upon rank of departed American soldiers. Right by the side of the stand where I spoke there was a little group of French women who had adopted those graves, had made themselves mothers of those dear ghosts by putting flowers every day upon those graves, taking them as their own sons, their own beloved, because they had died in the same cause – France was free and the world was free because America had come! I wish some men in public life who are now opposing the settlement for which these men died could visit such a spot as that. I wish that the thought that comes out of those graves could penetrate their consciousness. I wish that they could feel the moral obligation that rests upon us not to go back on those boys, but to see the thing through, to see it through to the end and make good their redemption of the world. For nothing less depends upon this decision, nothing less than the liberation and salvation of the world.

You will say, 'Is the League an absolute guarantee against war?' No; I do not know any absolute guarantee against the errors of human judgment or the violence of human passion, but I tell you this: With a cooling space of nine months for human passion, not much of it will keep hot. I had a couple of friends who were in the habit of losing their tempers, and when they lost their tempers they were in the habit of using very unparliamentary language. Some of their friends induced them to make a promise that they never would swear inside the town limits. When the impulse next came upon them, they took a street car to go out of town to swear, and by the time they got out of town they did not want to swear. They came back convinced that they were just what they were, a couple of unspeakable fools, and the habit of getting angry and of swearing suffered great inroads upon it by that experience. Now, illustrating the great by the small, that is true of the passions of nations. It is true of the passions of men however you combine them. Give them space to cool off. I ask you this: If it is not an absolute insurance against war, do you want no insurance at all? Do you want nothing? Do you want not only no probability that war will not recur, but the probability that it will recur? The arrangements of justice do not stand of themselves, my fellow citizens. The arrangements of this treaty are just, but they need the support of the combined power of the great nations of the world. And they will have that support. Now that the mists of this great question have cleared away, I believe that men will see the truth, eye to eye and face to face. There is one thing that the American people always rise to and extend their hand to, and that is the truth of justice and of liberty and of peace. We have accepted that truth and we are going to be led by it, and it is going to lead us, and through us the world, out into pastures of quietness and peace such as the world never dreamed of before.

'Address Delivered on Western Tour: At Pueblo, Colorado, September 25, 1919.' *The Public Papers of Woodrow Wilson: War and Peace*, ed. Ray Stannard Baker and William E. Dodd (2 vols., New York, 1927), II, pp. 399-416

SELECT BIBLIOGRAPHY

IMPERIALISM AND THE WAR WITH SPAIN

Beisner, Robert L., *Twelve Against Empire: The Anti-imperialists, 1898–1900* (New York, 1968)

Dulles, Foster Rhea, *The Imperial Years* (New York, 1956)

LaFeber, Walter, *The New Empire: An Interpretation of American Expansion, 1860–1898* (Ithaca, N.Y., 1963)

May, Ernest R., *American Imperialism: A Speculative Essay* (New York, 1968)

May, Ernest R., *Imperial Democracy* (New York, 1961)

Morgan, H. Wayne, *America's Road to Empire: The War with Spain and Overseas Expansion* (New York, 1965)

Neale, R. G., *Great Britain and United States Expansion: 1898–1900* (East Lansing, Mich., 1966)

Pratt, Julius W., *America's Colonial Experiment* (New York, 1950)

Pratt, Julius W., *Expansionists of 1898* (Baltimore, 1936)

THE UNITED STATES AND THE FAR EAST

Bailey, Thomas A., *Theodore Roosevelt and the Japanese-American Crises* (Stanford, 1934)

Dennett, Tyler, *Roosevelt and the Russo-Japanese War* (Garden City, N.Y., 1925)

Esthus, Raymond A., *Theodore Roosevelt and Japan* (Seattle, 1966)

Griswold, A. Whitney, *The Far Eastern Policy of the United States* (New Haven, 1938)

Neu, Charles E., *An Uncertain Friendship: Theodore Roosevelt and Japan, 1906–1909* (Cambridge, Mass., 1967)

Treat, Payson J., *Diplomatic Relations Between the United States and Japan, 1895–1905* (Stanford, 1938)

Varg, Paul A., *Open Door Diplomat: The Life of W. W. Rockhill* (Urbana, Ill., 1952)

Vevier, Charles, *The United States and China, 1906–1913* (New Brunswick, N.J., 1955)

White, John Albert, *The Diplomacy of the Russo-Japanese War* (Princeton, 1964)

THE UNITED STATES AND LATIN AMERICA

Bemis, Samuel Flagg, *The Latin American Policy of the United States* (New York, 1943)

Callcott, Wilfrid A., *The Caribbean Policy of the United States, 1890–1920* (Baltimore, 1942)

Calvert, Peter, *The Mexican Revolution, 1910–1914: The Diplomacy of Anglo-American Conflict* (Cambridge, England, 1968)

Cline, Howard F., *The United States and Mexico* (rev. ed. Cambridge, Mass., 1963).

Healy, David F., *The United States in Cuba, 1898–1902* (Madison, Wis., 1963)

Link, Arthur S., *Wilson: The New Freedom* (Princeton, 1956)

Munro, Dana G., *Intervention and Dollar Diplomacy in the Caribbean, 1900–1921* (Princeton, 1964)

Perkins, Dexter, *A History of the Monroe Doctrine* (rev. ed. Boston, 1955)

Quirk, Robert E., *An Affair of Honor: Woodrow Wilson and the Occupation of Veracruz* (Lexington, Ky., 1962)

THE UNITED STATES AND EUROPE

Allen, H. C., *Great Britain and the United States* (London, 1955)

Beale, Howard K., *Theodore Roosevelt and the Rise of America to World Power* (Baltimore, 1956)

Campbell, Alexander E., *Great Britain and the United States, 1895–1903* (London, 1960)

Campbell, Jr., Charles S., *Anglo-American Understanding, 1898–1903* (Baltimore, 1957)

Davis, Calvin DeArmond, *The United States and the First Hague Peace Conference* (Ithaca, N.Y., 1962)

Dennett, Tyler, *John Hay* (New York, 1933)

Gelber, Lionel M., *The Rise of Anglo-American Friendship: A Study in World Politics, 1898–1906* (London, 1936)

Heindel, Richard H., *The American Impact on Great Britain, 1898–1914* (Philadelphia, 1940)

Perkins, Bradford, *The Great Rapprochement: England and the United States, 1895–1914* (New York, 1968)

THE ROAD TO WAR

Birnbaum, Karl E., *Peace Moves and U-Boat Warfare* (Stockholm, 1958)

Buehrig, Edward H., *Woodrow Wilson and the Balance of Power* (Bloomington, Ind., 1955)

Fischer, Fritz, *Germany's Aims in the First World War* (New York, 1967)

Link, Arthur S., *Wilson: Campaigns for Progressivism and Peace, 1916–1917* (Princeton, 1965)

Link, Arthur S., *Wilson: Confusion and Crises, 1915–1916* (Princeton, 1964)

Link, Arthur S., *Wilson the Diplomatist* (Baltimore, 1957)

Link, Arthur S., *Wilson: The Struggle for Neutrality, 1914–1915* (Princeton, 1960)

May, Ernest R., *The World War and American Isolation, 1914–1917* (Cambridge, Mass., 1959)

Seymour, Charles, *American Neutrality, 1914–1917* (New Haven, 1935)

Spindler, Arno, *Der Handelskrieg mit U-booten* (3 vols., Berlin, 1932–1934)

THE FIRST WORLD WAR AND VERSAILLES

Bailey, Thomas A., *Woodrow Wilson and the Great Betrayal* (New York, 1945)

Bailey, Thomas A., *Woodrow Wilson and the Lost Peace* (New York, 1944)

Birdsall, Paul, *Versailles Twenty Years After* (New York, 1941)

Fleming, Denna F., *The United States and the League of Nations, 1918–1920* (New York, 1932)

Gelfand, Lawrence E., *The Inquiry: American Preparations for Peace, 1917–1919* (New Haven, 1963)

Kennan, George F., *The Decision to Intervene* (Princeton, 1958)

Kennan, George F., *Russia Leaves the War* (Princeton, 1956)

Levin, Jr., N. Gordon, *Woodrow Wilson and World Politics: America's Response to War and Revolution* (New York, 1968)

Martin, Laurence W., *Peace Without Victory: Woodrow Wilson and the British Liberals* (New Haven, 1958)

Mayer, Arno J., *Political Origins of the New Diplomacy, 1917–1918* (New Haven, 1959)

Mayer, Arno J., *Politics and Diplomacy of Peacemaking: Containment and Counter-revolution at Versailles, 1918–1919* (New York, 1967)

Rudin, Harry R., *Armistice, 1918* (New Haven, 1944)

Thompson, John M., *Russia, Bolshevism, and the Versailles Peace* (Princeton, 1966)

Tillman, Seth P., *Anglo-American Relations at the Paris Peace Conference of 1919* (Princeton, 1961)

Unterberger, Betty M., *America's Siberian Expedition, 1918–1920* (Durham, N.C., 1956)

Yates, Louis A. R., *The United States and French Security, 1917–1921* (New York, 1957)